DRAGONS & FANTASY

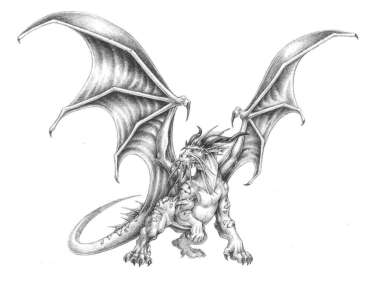

By Kythera of Anevern

Walter Foster

CONTENTS

Brimming with creative inspiration, how-to projects, and useful information to enrich your everyday life, Quarto Knows is a favorite destination for those pursuing their interests and passions. Visit our site and dig deeper with our books into your area of interest: Quarto Creates, Quarto Cooks, Quarto Homes, Quarto Lives, Quarto Drives, Quarto Explores, Quarto Gifts, or Quarto Kids.

First Published in 2009 by Walter Foster Publishing, an imprint of The Quarto Group.
26391 Crown Valley Parkway, Suite 220, Mission Viejo, CA 92691, USA.
T (949) 380-7510 F (949) 380-7575 www.QuartoKnows.com

Walter Foster Publishing titles are also available at discount for retail, wholesale, promotional, and bulk purchase. For details, contact the Special Sales Manager by email at specialsales@quarto.com or by mail at The Quarto Group, Attn: Special Sales Manager, 100 Cummings Center, Suite 265D, Beverly, MA 01915, USA.

ISBN: 978-1-60058-068-0

Printed in China
20 19

INTRODUCTION

The world we live in, though mundane, is a wonderful place, full of marvels in our past and present. Part of our history, however, lies in the fantastic. The human imagination stretches beyond the limits of the things that we can see and touch—fairies, dragons, elves, and other creatures of all shapes and sizes have had a place in our culture for centuries, being found in everything from myths and legends to songs and art. The challenge contemporary artists face is bringing the fantastic to life on the page, breathing life into the mythical with graphite, paint, ink, or pixels on a computer screen.

Most art instruction begins with drawing what you see, translating the world around you into lines on a page. With practice, this becomes easy enough because we can see these things and learn how to mimic their shapes and textures on paper. But what about the things we can't see, the fabulous creatures that are conjured up by the most far-flung corners of our imagination?

After months of struggling with the challenge of making my fantasy creatures look believable, I finally came to the realization that the tools for creating the fantastic have their roots in the mundane. As much as I didn't want to draw vases of flowers, dolls, and lemons in dishes, I figured out that I had to be able to find the ordinary in the extraordinary to make my fantasy creatures come to life on the page.

Of course, what works for me might not work for you because everyone thinks (and draws) differently. The trick is figuring out what works for you. I hope the methods and techniques I describe in this book will be a good starting point for you—a basis from which to cultivate your own methods and techniques. Heck, I've been doing this for years and I still remain in a constant state of evaluation, always reconsidering my techniques and my ways of thinking.

So keep one eye on the stars (anything is possible), but keep the other on the horizon, where you might catch a glimpse of something that helps bring the fantastic just a little bit closer. You never know when you might see a dragon in a cat ferociously chasing a mouse, or a wine-drenched satyr in an iguana basking on a sunlit branch.

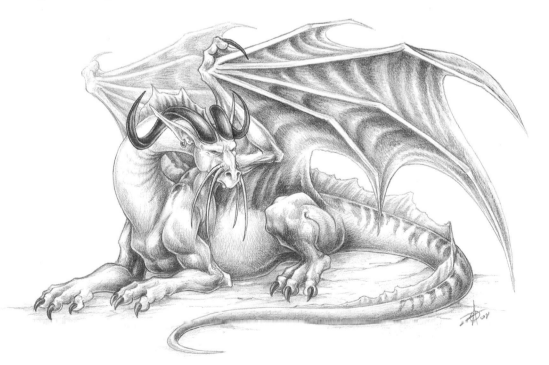

TOOLS AND MATERIALS

There are many types of tools and materials available for an artist to use. On the other hand, sometimes walking into a large art supply store can result in sensory overload, and you're left wondering if you really need all of the amazing things on the shelves. All of these tools have potential and can be a lot of fun, but let's start with the basics. Experiment as much as you can to discover which tools work best for you.

▶ **Pencils** Wood-cased drawing pencils are available in varying degrees of hardness, from very hard (9H) to very soft (9B); HB pencils are used for middle grades. The higher the number that accompanies the letter, the harder or softer the lead. (For example, a 4H is harder than a 2H, and a 4B is softer than a 2B.) You can buy woodless pencils, which also come in varying degrees and are great for covering large areas with tone or for making quick sketches. My favorite sketching tool is a mechanical pencil, which can be loaded with graphite leads of different sizes. I almost never heave home without my .5 mm and .7 mm HB mechanical pencils. Clutch pencils are similar to mechanical pencils but hold only one thicker 2 mm lead, which is ideal for broad strokes. Know that tones vary among manufacturers—one brand's HB may look very different from another brand's, so try to stick with one brand for consistency.

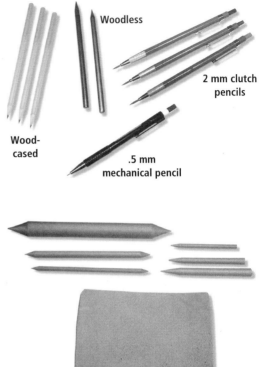

Woodless

2 mm clutch pencils

Wood-cased

.5 mm mechanical pencil

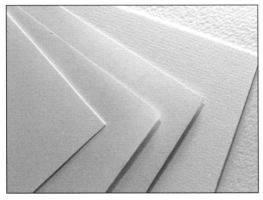

Paper Drawing paper comes in different sizes and textures. Some textures are better suited to certain materials than others: When working in graphite, a paper that has some texture (tooth) is preferable, because the graphite adheres better; when working with pen and ink, smoother paper is usually better. Experiment with different kinds of paper to see how your drawing materials react. Just make sure your paper is acid free, as this paper will last for a long time and won't yellow with age.

Blending Tools These tools can be used to help blend the graphite on the page. Blending stumps (above left) are sticks of highly compressed paper pulp. Like pencils, they wear down as they are used, but you can restore a blunt point by carefully sanding the point with fine-grain sandpaper. Tortillons (above right) function much the same as blending stumps, but they are made of tightly rolled paper. For large areas, blend with a chamois cloth (above center). You can wrap the chamois around your finger for best results. Never use just your finger to blend as the natural oils in your skin can damage the paper.

▶ **Light Table** A light table (also called a "light box") is a great tool for transferring a messy sketch to good paper. Tape your sketch to the surface of the light table, cover the sketch with a clean sheet of drawing paper, and flip the switch—the fluorescent bulb illuminates your drawing and will help you accurately trace the lines of the sketch onto a nice sheet of drawing paper. You can get the same effect by taping your sketch and drawing paper to a bright window, but this will only work during the day.

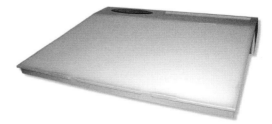

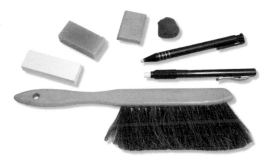

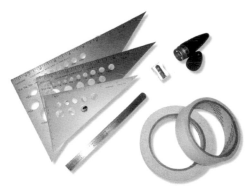

Erasers Erasers can be used to correct mistakes, create visual effects, and even draw! The white plastic eraser (above left) is smooth, simple, and more or less all-purpose. The next eraser, a gum eraser, is softer but has a tendency to crumble and leave a mess if used too roughly. The next two are kneaded erasers—these can be molded into different shapes and sizes, as shown. Instead of rubbing the eraser on the page as you would with a plastic or gum eraser, gently dab the kneaded eraser on the page to lift the graphite. The last two stick erasers are similar to clutch pencils in that they each hold a single white plastic eraser "stick." The soft brush pictured here is useful for brushing away eraser crumbs. You can smear the graphite or damage the paper if you use your hand, and you might end up with a wet drawing if you try to blow away the crumbs.

Other Tools Drawing isn't just about pencils and erasers. I use artists' triangles for measuring and drawing borders; I also like to keep a small ruler on hand for drawing straight lines in smaller areas. Pencil sharpeners are essential if you are using wood-cased or woodless pencils. You can purchase special sharpeners for mechanical leads. A traditional hand-held sharpener is pictured here, along with a sharpener that has a reservoir to catch pencil shavings. This particular sharpener also has a cap that keeps smaller pencil shavings and graphite dust from escaping and making a mess. You might also find it helpful to keep artist's tape on hand for securing your drawings to a surface or creating clean borders and edges (see page 62). Artist's tape is easy to peel off and won't leave a sticky residue when you remove it like masking tape does.

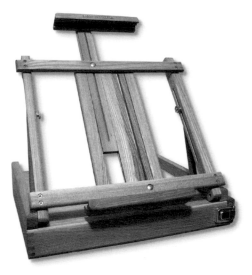

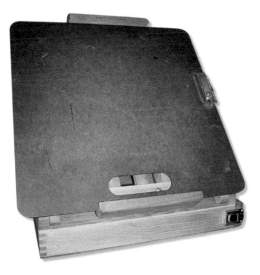

Easel I don't have the luxury of a large workspace. To make up for this, I have a small, adjustable tabletop easel. This particular easel has a drawer incorporated into the base, which is great for storing tools. My easel is about the size of a briefcase and has a carrying handle and wood brackets for holding paper in place.

Drawing Board I also have a drawing board, which I use as a drawing surface for my easel. You can use any smooth, hard, flat surface as a drawing board, but this store-bought one is my favorite because it fits nicely on the easel and accommodates the smaller size of paper I prefer to work with.

DRAWING AND SHADING TECHNIQUES

To make something look convincing and three-dimensional on two-dimensional paper, you need to give the object form by adding highlights and shadows. If you aren't familiar with shading methods, here are some techniques to get you started. It's a good idea to practice some of these techniques to get the hang of them before you apply them to a drawing. Don't be afraid to experiment and be adventurous, though; these are just a few ideas to get you started. You might want to line up some household items (such as fruit, bowls, and bottles) on a tabletop and try to sketch them as they are. This is good practice for helping you learn how highlights and shadows fall on items of different shapes and sizes.

Hatching This shading technique involves placing several lines parallel to one another. Lighter, widely spaced lines create lighter areas; darker, more dense lines create dark areas. Note that the lines in this example do not form identifiable rows. You can achieve a smoother look by mixing up where each line starts and stops.

Crosshatching The addition of another layer of hatching, placed at an angle, is called "crosshatching." As with hatching, lighter, widely spaced lines create light areas, whereas denser areas create darks. An advantage of crosshatching is that the direction of your lines can be used to define the shape of an object.

Gradating This technique creates smooth, graduated values (from dark to light). Start with a soft pencil to lay down darker layers; then use harder pencils and less pressure for progressively lighter tones. Going back over the edges of your dark areas with a slightly harder pencil can help blend the shadows into the lighter areas.

Scribbling This is a fast, effective way to shade when sketching. When applied with patience and diligence, it can also work effectively in finished drawings. Loose, light scribble lines create lighter areas, whereas thicker, darker lines define darker areas. Switch between hard and soft pencils to keep your lights light and your darks darker.

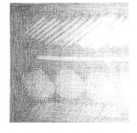

Blending with a Stump The bottom half of this gradated example has been blended using a blending stump (see page 4). By rubbing the blending stump over the shaded areas, you can smooth the shading and create various looks.

Blending with a Chamois The bottom half of this example has been blended using a small piece of chamois leather, which is very soft and can be purchased in different sizes. Chamois squares can come in handy for blending very large areas, such as expansive skies, or other background elements that will be built up with other marks and eraser techniques.

Erasing Erasers can be used for more than just correcting mistakes. I use a stick eraser to draw the hatchmarks at the top of this example, and a kneaded eraser to lift out blotches of graphite from the bottom. Try using erasers to bring out details in shaded areas, or to draw lighter shapes into dark areas. Just be mindful as to how much graphite the eraser can lift.

Stippling This technique of using small dots to define shape and shadows can be very time consuming. It is best done with softer pencils that aren't quite sharpened to a point, and without using a great deal of pressure. A point that is too sharp or applied with too much pressure can leave pockmarks in your paper.

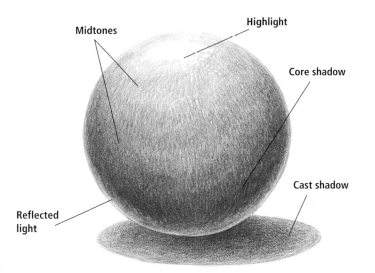

Midtones

Highlight

Core shadow

Cast shadow

Reflected light

Shading Exercise Shading a sphere is a simple yet useful exercise for developing shading skills and techniques, and for locating the different types of highlights and shadows on an object. Variations of this exercise can be used to shade just about anything, allowing you to give your drawings form and volume. In this example, I use a combination of gradating and hatching with lines that follow the curve of the sphere to achieve a smooth texture that also shows the shape of the object. First shade the sphere with a very light tone, leaving the white of the paper at a spot near the top of the sphere (though not quite at the edge). This white spot is the *highlight*—the area where the light shines brightest on the object. Next build up layers of darker tones as you reach the bottom of the sphere. Even though you are building up the shading in layers, it is important to try to blend each layer smoothly into the previous layer. Eventually, the darkest shadows should be in a thin band around the base of the object, leaving a range of *midtones* (middle values) between the highlight and the darkest area, which is the *core shadow*. Note that the core shadow does not extend all the way to the base of the object. Rather, there is a lighter band just below the core shadow—This is the *reflected light*. Even if a surface is not shiny, it will still reflect a small amount of light back onto the object resting on it. Below the sphere is the *cast shadow*—this is the shadow cast by the object itself. Notice that the cast shadow is not a solid tone; rather, it gets lighter as it moves away from the object.

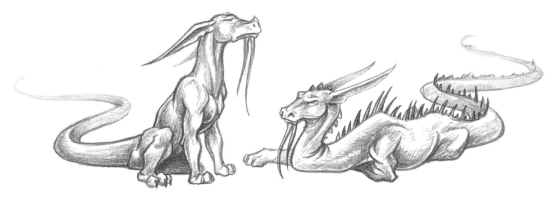

Using Atmospheric Perspective Once you have mastered the basics of shading, there are other techniques you can use to make objects look closer or farther away. Notice that in this example, the tail of the dragon on the left gets lighter as it extends from its body (just like the cast shadow in the sphere example above). This is called "atmospheric perspective"—the tendency of objects that are farther away to become lighter as they recede into the distance. This is easily observed if you live in an area with mountains—the farther away the mountains are, the lighter they get, until they almost blend into the sky. Note that this rule applies only to daytime drawings. If your drawing is a nighttime scene, the opposite is true—objects that are farther away are darker, and objects that are closer are lighter and more clearly defined. Diminishing levels of detail also help show distance. Notice that the tail and the spikes of the dragon on the right get smaller and less distinct as they get farther away. You can still tell that the spikes extend all the way down the dragon's tail, but they become less and less defined, showing the distance and making the drawing more convincing.

CREATURE FEATURES

Horns, wings, feathers, fur, claws: There are a lot of features and details to consider when designing your creatures! When drawing these features, keep in mind that it's often helpful to use photo references of animals or humans with features similar to those you want to add to your fantasy drawings. This page will help you experiment with creating textures such as smooth scales and ridged horns, as well as with depicting elements such as wings and tails. And if you're almost finished with a drawing and can't shake the feeling that something is missing, consider some of these options to give your creature that last bit of oomph.

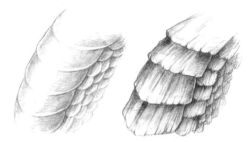

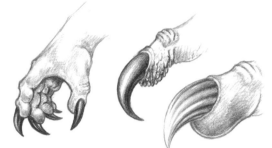

Scales Study existing scaly creatures, such as snakes, crocodiles, and even fish to get inspiration for scales. The scales above left are smooth and slick, like the belly of a snake. By keeping the shading light and blending away the edges of the scales where the lightest highlights are, the scales appear to be thin and flexible, like a fish. The scales above right, however, have very deep shading and are riddled with ridges, nicks, and cracks along the edges. These scales look very thick and hard—the sort that would make up the armor-like plates on an old, weathered dragon.

Claws Claws come in a wonderful variety of shapes and sizes and have many functions. Take a look at the examples in nature, such as tigers, eagles, lizards, and even dogs. Then think about the type of creature you are drawing and what purpose it might use its claws for. The example above left shows how long, thick talons might look on a gargoyle's hand—useful for attacking, defending, and climbing. The middle example could be found on the toes of a dragon or harpy. Based on an eagle's talon, this claw is good for hooking and grasping. The example above right is a good all-purpose claw with ridges.

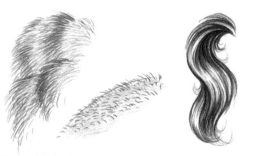

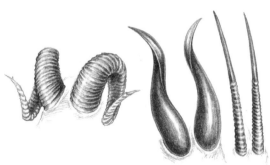

Fur and Hair When drawing short hair (above left), use medium-length strokes and avoid creating parallel rows, instead interspersing your lines and drawing them in the same general direction. Darker, denser lines can show stripes or other patterns and areas of shadow. Wiry, bristly hair (center) is drawn with short, quick pencil strokes. This is a good technique for drawing close-cropped hair or the stubble on an ogre's knuckles and toes. The long hair shown above right is good for manes and tails. Use long, smooth lines that follow the direction of hair growth. To make the hair look shiny, let some of the white paper show through in areas. Not all hair is the same length, so let some lines trail off into wisps or curls for a more natural look.

Horns As with the other examples on this page, you can find ideas for your creature's horns by modifying what you see in nature. Many animals have horns that are fantastically exotic, but something standard, like the curled ram horns above left, also works nicely for a range of fantasy creatures. Adding twists to smooth horns as in the middle example creates a refined look. In the above-right example, growth ridges can blend into smooth horn tips, creating a look that is both rough and dignified.

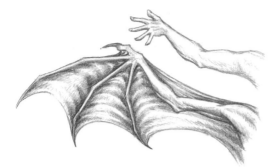

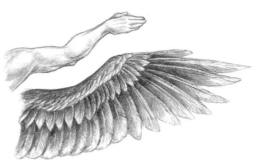

Leathery Wings Wings are, essentially, a second pair of arms and hands. The bones are thin and elongated, but the basic structure matches that of human hands and arms. Bats are the primary living example of this in that their forelimbs are their wings. In the example above, compare the "fingers" of the wing to the splayed fingers in the hand. Note that both limbs have a wrist, an elbow, a shoulder, and even a thumb. Keep this basic structure in mind, and then expand on it. Add more or fewer wing fingers, or consider long spikes that protrude from the elbow.

Feathered Wings Bird wings are also similar to human arms and hands. Unlike leathery wings where the wing is supported by elongated fingers, the "fingers" of a feathered wing are fused together. The feathers make up the bulk of the wing and give it its shape. Though feathers can be intimidating, you don't need to draw every individual feather. Emphasize the primary feathers—the long feathers that look almost like fingers along the outer edge of the wing—and use less definition for the smallest feathers on the top layer (though you should emphasize the outer edges and perhaps show some markings).

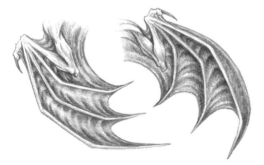

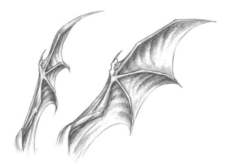

Folded Wings When not in flight, creatures usually fold their wings to keep them out of the way and to keep themselves safe. Folded wings can be held close to the body, or simply held low and relaxed. The membrane of wings—as with bats—is usually stretchy, even when relaxed. The examples above don't show too much slack, other than folds between the wing fingers; however, you can also draw wings with folds that run parallel to the wing fingers and hang a bit like drapes when relaxed.

Open Wings When wings are open, the membrane between the wing fingers stretches and is pulled tight. Some folds are present, but not too many. Note that the edge of the membrane has a smoother arc where it stretches between the wing fingers, instead of the steep arc that occurs with folded wings. The example above left shows an open wing that is tilted away from the viewer.

▶ **Expressive Wings** Creatures are quite attached to their wings. When extra limbs are naturally part of a creature's anatomy, they will come into play as another means of expressing that creature's thoughts and feelings through body language. In this example, the dragon on the right is clearly agitated, spreading his wings to make himself look bigger and more intimidating. The dragon on the left is cowed by the other dragon's display of aggression and is tucking his wings in close, as if to cower behind them in a submissive, non-threatening pose.

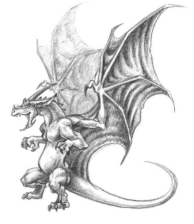

TYPES OF DRAGONS

Ultimately, there are as many different types of dragons as there are people who want to draw them. Size, shape, texture, details—all of these things are up to the artist, and there's no limit to what you can come up with. However, in terms of the dragons that are described in classic myths and stories, there are several specific types of dragons that show up quite often. Here are four of these types, which I present as a place for you to start cultivating ideas.

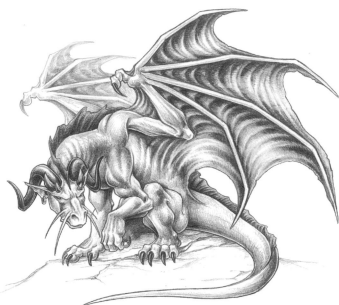

◄ **Western (Classic) Dragon** In Western culture, this type of dragon is the most familiar: terrorizing kingdoms, dueling with knights, and kidnapping young princesses. Occasionally they appear as good guys, providing strength or wisdom, or as the patron who serves the heroes with their quest. Their reputation is mixed at best, but they remain a beloved archetype. Western dragons usually have four limbs; the forelimbs may or may not end in hand-like paws. Most have two wings, horns, a long tail, and spiky ridges or fins running along the spine.

▶ **Eastern Dragon** Whereas dragons often play the role of the villain in Western culture, Eastern dragons are usually respected and considered wise and benevolent. They can, of course, be angered, but are not usually envisioned as being predisposed to unfounded rage or unprovoked antagonism, as are their Western cousins. Unlike Western dragons, Eastern dragons usually do not have wings. Rather, their bodies are very long and slender, and their flight is marked by writhing, coiling movements. They usually have four limbs, with the number of claws on each foot varying according to the type of dragon (and sometimes their rank or status). Their horns usually resemble the antlers of a deer.

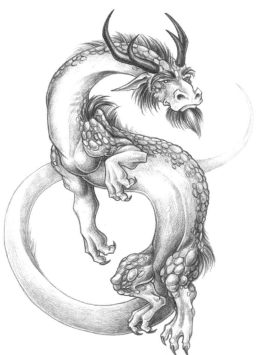

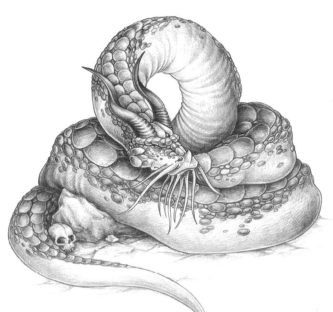

◄ **Wyrm** The wyrm (pronounced "worm") is a type of dragon with no legs or wings. The word can also refer to dragons in general, or specify that a dragon is very old. But for our purposes, the term refers to limbless dragons. There are many examples of wyrms in mythology, such as Jörmungandr, the World Serpent from Norse mythology who grew so long that he could wrap himself around the Earth and grasp the end of his tail in his mouth. Because wyrms lack wings and limbs, other means must be used to make them look like dragons: Try using thick scales or ridges along the length of its body. The best place to focus on, of course, is the creature's head: Add horns, whiskers, bumps, brow ridges, fins, or perhaps even long ears.

► **Wyvern** The wyvern is another type of dragon, often regarded as vicious and foul-tempered, and sometimes less intelligent than the Western dragon. The exact appearance of wyverns varies slightly from story to story. Most commonly, they have two wings and two hind legs. Like bats, their forelimbs function as their wings. Sometimes their tail ends in a spade, other times in a sharp barb, which is usually poisonous. In this example, I've given the creature lots of wicked-looking horns and spikes to make it look malevolent.

CLASSIC DRAGON

One of the most archetypal creatures of myth, legend, and contemporary fantasy, the dragon has terrified and fascinated humankind throughout history. Classical literature and myths of old will provide you with some of the most standard descriptions of a dragon's appearance: broad wings, spiky horns, fearsome teeth, rending claws, long tails, and thick skin or dense, armored scales. But there are as many different types of dragons as your imagination can conjure up, so once you have the hang of drawing a classic dragon, experiment with different looks and features to make your own unique creatures.

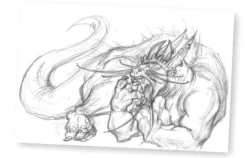

Unusual Expressions There's more to dragons than blind savagery and ferocity. They can be silly too! Try experimenting with different moods and situations, including the unusual. This dragon makes an action as mundane as yawning seem impressive.

Creating Character

▶ **Eyes** Like humans, a dragon's eyes can speak volumes about its personality. Slanted reptilian eyes suggest a cold, savage personality; large, thoughtful eyes produce an intelligent or kindly look.

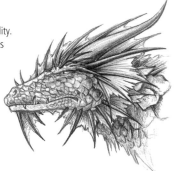

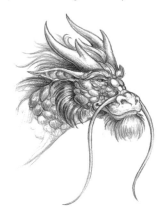

◀ **Horns and Whiskers** Features like horns and whiskers can help suggest a dragon's age and personality. An older dragon might have a broken or cracked horn, and a dragon with vast treasures might don an earring or two. Long, drooping whiskers suggest old age.

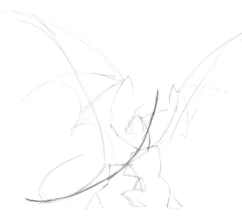

◀ **Step 1** I begin all of my drawings on a sheet of sketch paper. With an HB pencil, I establish the *line of action*, which is usually a single line that indicates the general flow of the figure. Then I use quick lines to rough in the shapes of the dragon's body and wings, remembering that the wingspan should appear to be about twice the dragon's length. Starting with a rough sketch like this helps me determine the placement of the figure on the page and work out the composition before I get too involved. I don't worry about details at this point—just the general shapes.

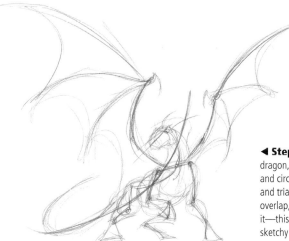

◄ Step 2 Once I'm happy with the pose and placement of my dragon, I start developing the figure with basic shapes: ovals and circles for the cranium and ribcage, cylinders for the limbs, and triangular wedges for the feet. When limbs or body masses overlap, I sketch the farther limb through the one in front of it—this is called "drawing through." Note that my lines are very sketchy and loose at this stage.

► Step 3 Now I start building up specific muscle masses and adding a little more detail, still drawing very loose sketch lines with the HB pencil. At this stage, I start to flesh out the wings, adding more definition to the joints and sketching the wing membrane, making the edges curve between the "fingers" of the wing to suggest tension. Note how the wings join the body—they connect along the length of the back to the base of the tail, much like bat wings. This makes the wing surface appear greater.

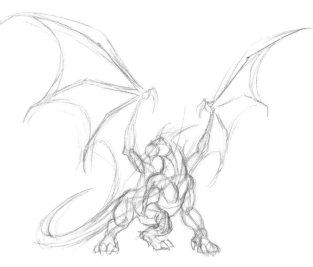

◄ Step 4 At this point, I erase any unneeded lines and emphasize those I want to keep. I use the HB pencil to start adding more details, such as the face, ears (including an earring), whiskers, horns, and claws. I switch to a slightly harder H pencil for the smaller details.

► **Step 5** This is the stage in the drawing process where I transfer my drawing from the sketch paper to a sheet of art paper (usually Bristol paper). I do this by tracing the image with the help of a light table and an HB pencil. This allows me to ignore all the lines I don't want and make the lines I do want as clean and neat as possible. After my sketch is transferred, I use HB and H pencils to begin adding light tone to areas of the wings and body by layering soft strokes and some hatching—especially in the wings. I make the dragon's lower belly and hind leg the darkest, as they are in shadow. I also add a few new details, such as the claws at the tips of the wing "fingers" and the spiky crest that extends from the back of the dragon's head to the base of the tail. Then I lightly indicate areas where I want to place markings on the dragon's legs, back, and tail.

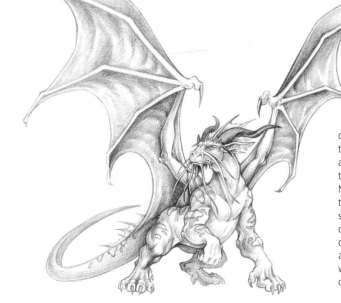

◄ **Step 6** I am completely satisfied with my lines, so I continue using the HB pencil and a 2B to shade the wings, body, and face, using more pressure for the deepest shadows. I prefer to shade all over the drawing, building up from light to dark, rather than work on separate areas until they're finished. I find that this results in a more unified drawing. Next I add the iris and pupil, and I shade the horns and crest. I also deepen the shading in the wings to suggest folds. I don't want the wings to look too deeply creased, however, as this dragon's wings are spread open. It's helpful to study bat wings when adding form and volume to dragon wings.

► **Step 7** I'm on the home stretch now! With 3B and 4B pencils, I build up the shadows in layers, making the darkest areas even darker and adding more definition in the details, such as the facial features, horns, claws, and the markings on the body. I keep the shading on the end of the tail and the hind foot lighter and flatter, using atmospheric perspective—the tendency of receding objects to appear lighter and less detailed—to suggest distance.

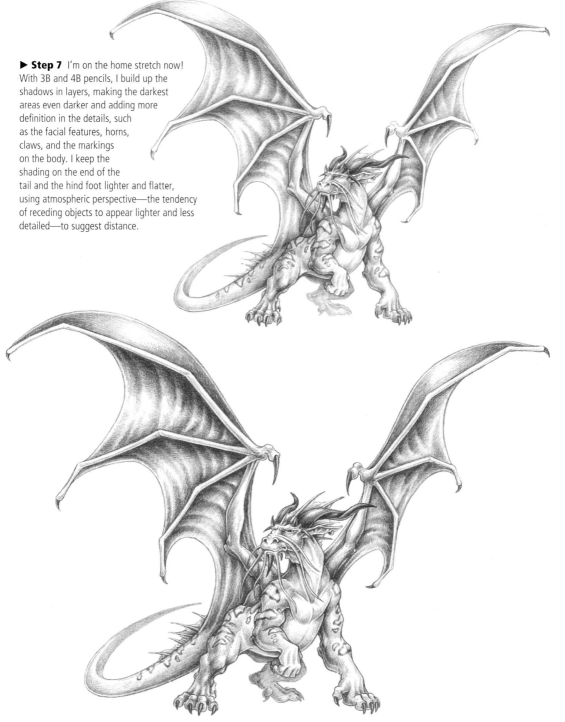

Step 8 To finish the drawing, I emphasize the dark areas with a softer 6B pencil and blend some of the shadows by layering and building up more strokes with harder HB and B pencils. I use a kneaded eraser to lift out highlights in the folds of the wings, on the horns and claws, and within the dragon's skin markings. When I'm satisfied with the range of values and areas of contrast, my dragon is ready to take flight.

EASTERN DRAGON

Dragons are not unique to Western culture, of course—Japan and China are rife with tales and paintings of dragons, usually depicted as benevolent and wise beings, often respected and revered as guardian spirits. Perhaps the most striking difference between dragons of the East and dragons of the West is their appearance. Eastern dragons have long, serpentine bodies, and they do not have wings; however, they achieve flight by floating and undulating through the air. Eastern dragons are often depicted with beards, thick manes, two elk- or deerlike horns, and long whiskers, like a catfish or carp. This lesson will demonstrate drawing the general characteristics of Eastern dragons so you can capture their essence in your own drawings.

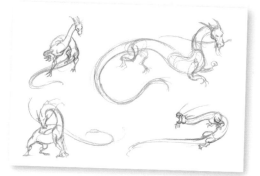

Rough Sketches Eastern dragons present a range of drawing possibilities. Because they do not have wings, there is more freedom—and perhaps a greater challenge—in using their unique body type in the composition of the drawing. Spend some time creating rough sketches, and try not to get caught up in a repetition of S curves. Overlapping the dragon's coils can help create a sense of depth.

▶ **Step 1** I begin by drawing the line of action with an HB pencil. I sketch separate lines to indicate the coil shape of the dragon's body; then I rough in lines for the legs. I sketch some rough forms to develop more areas of the body as this helps me find a pleasing composition. Without wings to fill up the frame, there is more freedom to play around with the coil-shaped body, neck, and tail.

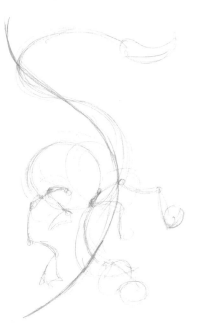

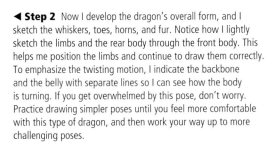

◀ **Step 2** Now I develop the dragon's overall form, and I sketch the whiskers, toes, horns, and fur. Notice how I lightly sketch the limbs and the rear body through the front body. This helps me position the limbs and continue to draw them correctly. To emphasize the twisting motion, I indicate the backbone and the belly with separate lines so I can see how the body is turning. If you get overwhelmed by this pose, don't worry. Practice drawing simpler poses until you feel more comfortable with this type of dragon, and then work your way up to more challenging poses.

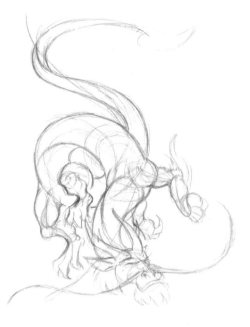

◄ **Step 3** I'm happy with this composition, so I continue using the HB pencil to develop the form by outlining specific muscle masses. I add more detail to the toes and fur, as well as a few facial features, such as brow ridges and nostrils. I also more clearly define the shape of the visible ear.

▶ **Step 4** Using the HB pencil, I clean up extra sketch lines I don't need and darken the lines I want to keep. I further outline the muscle masses and start defining more specific details, including the claws, eyes, horns, and other facial features. Notice the faint outline of the sphere this dragon is holding. Some legends mention Eastern dragons possessing a giant "pearl of wisdom." Details like this are up to you, but I like the idea of this dragon carrying its favorite bauble.

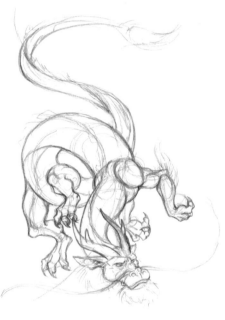

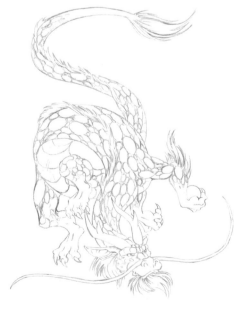

◄ **Step 5** I transfer my sketch to a sheet of heavier drawing paper so my lines are as clean as possible. I also completely erase the remaining sketch lines I don't want. I further define details, such as claws, horns, and hair, including the mane that travels down the ridge of the spine. By far the most dramatic jump between this step and the previous step is the addition of scales, which I sketch lightly with my trusty HB pencil. Because I've transferred my drawing to a fresh sheet of paper, I don't add the scales until the lines are as clean as possible. If you find it easier to add the scales sooner, by all means do so!

▶ **Step 6** Now that I've added the scales, I start laying down some basic shading using short strokes and hatching with the lighter H pencil; this helps add volume to the dragon's limbs and muscle masses. I work the whole image before developing the shading any further. This way I'll have a better idea of how the shading will work throughout the image, and I can see which areas need deeper shadows or additional highlights.

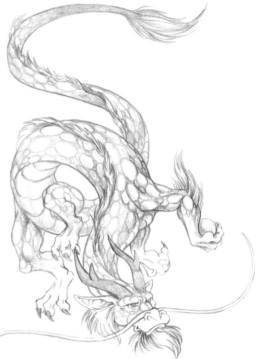

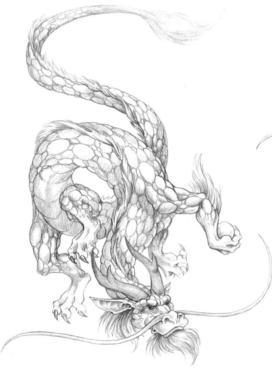

◀ **Step 7** To develop more shading throughout the drawing, I lay down midtones and establish where some of the darker shadows will be by layering shorter, soft strokes using B and 2B pencils. I gradually reduce the detail along the dragon's tail using atmospheric perspective to make it seem farther away.

Drawing Scales

Scales have the potential to be the most challenging aspect of drawing dragons; however, the process can also be the most rewarding when you find a method that works for you. For this project, I've chosen an irregular pattern of scales that look somewhat "pebbly." I'm fond of the unusual look it produces when combined with smooth belly scales, like those on a snake. Experiment until you find a style that works best for you!

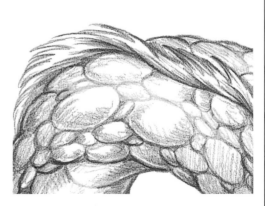

◄ Step 8 Once I establish where I want the deep shadows to be, I build them up using a combination of long and short strokes and some hatching with softer 3B and 4B pencils. Then, using soft strokes with the HB pencil, I blend the shadows into the midtones. Next I lift out highlights with a kneaded eraser. Shading the edges of the scales with a soft pencil and lightening the opposite edges with a kneaded eraser adds volume to the scales and helps shape the muscles underneath them. I also use the kneaded eraser to lift out highlights on the dragon's horns, as well as in the beard and mane.

FAIRY

Whether good or bad, humanlike or ethereal, winged or wingless, or large or small, fairies have been popular in myths and folklore for ages. Much of the folklore that surrounds fairies tells of their mischievous behavior, which includes tangling hair and disorienting travelers. A fairy can bestow gifts on a human child, but meddling in human affairs is one of their favorite hobbies!

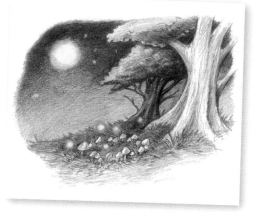

▶ **Fairy Atmospheres** Rural, moonlit forest hillsides and "fairy rings"—circles of mushrooms or toadstools like the one pictured here—are common settings in fairy lore.

◀ **Step 1** I start by drawing the line of action with an HB pencil, and then I indicate the rest of the body, including the wings, using basic shapes.

▶ **Step 2** Still using the HB pencil, I develop the body's form using more basic shapes—circles, ovals, and cylinders. Because I know how I want to position the hands, I sketch simple lines to delineate the fingers.

Fairy Wings

If you're looking for inspiration when drawing fairy wings, spend some time studying insects—dragonflies, butterflies, and even beetles—to get ideas. Also take note of leaves and try to incorporate their shapes into your wing designs.

◄ Step 3 I add more definition to the shapes and curves of the body. Then I start adding more details: I give more definition to the fingers; add long, pointy ears; and start sketching the hair and clothing. Because this fairy is from the wild forest, I add veins to the wings to make them look leaflike.

► Step 4 I clean up most of the sketch lines so I can focus on adding more of the fine details, such as facial features and jewelry. I also add more definition to the shirt, loincloth, and edges of the wings.

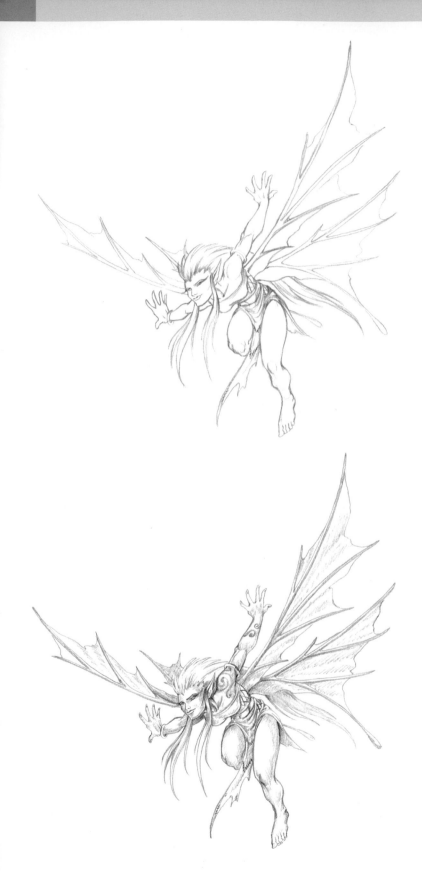

◄ Step 5 With the help of a light table and a lighter H pencil, I transfer my drawing to a clean sheet of Bristol paper. Once my fairy is on a clean page, I refine the details further. I add long eyelashes, and some stitching and lacing to the clothes. I also draw the full, flowing hair.

◄ Step 6 Using a combination of H and HB pencils, I shade the entire drawing using short, smooth strokes and hatching, which is especially evident in the folds of the wings and clothing. I avoid using hatching on the hair; instead, I use strokes that follow the flow of the hair, layering them in areas that are darker or in shadow. Where the hair falls behind the fairy's wings, I use atmospheric perspective—less detail and a general lighter tone throughout—to make the hair look as though it is blowing off the back. I also add a few more details, including the spirals painted on her shoulder and arm.

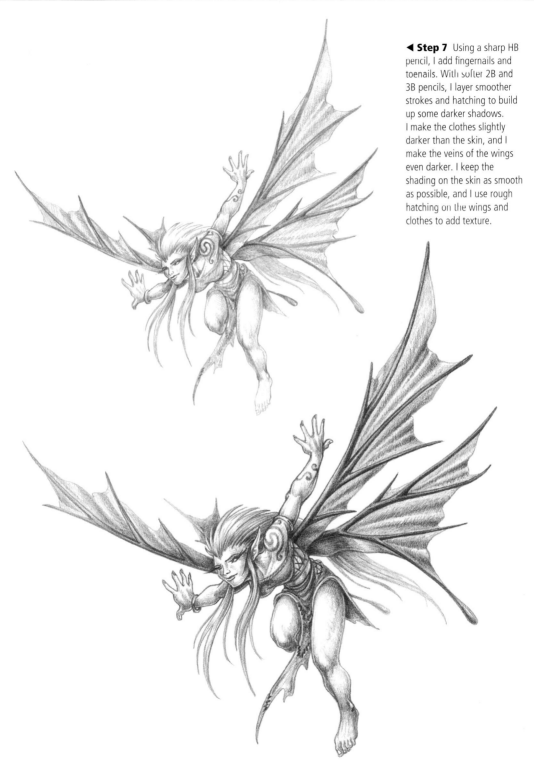

◄ Step 7 Using a sharp HB pencil, I add fingernails and toenails. With softer 2B and 3B pencils, I layer smoother strokes and hatching to build up some darker shadows. I make the clothes slightly darker than the skin, and I make the veins of the wings even darker. I keep the shading on the skin as smooth as possible, and I use rough hatching on the wings and clothes to add texture.

Step 8 I use a 4B pencil to build up the darkest shadows, and then I blend them into the highlights with the HB pencil. Using a kneaded eraser, I lift out highlights and gradually lighten the wing farthest from the body from base to tip (atmospheric perspective again). I also use the kneaded eraser to lighten the areas of the body paint that don't fall into shadow; as a result, the lines seem to follow the contour of the arm. I darken the lacing and stitching on the clothes so they stand out from the darker cloth and also match the darker shading of the veins on the wings. I finish shading the jewelry, face, and ears. Now this fairy is ready to make mischief!

GARGOYLE

Perched high on rooftops and cornices, gargoyles silently watch the world below, protecting their buildings by scaring away evil spirits with their grotesque features. Because of their monstrous appearance, gargoyles are often misinterpreted as evil creatures, rather than staunch guardians. In mythology, gargoyles either turn to stone at will or by force in daylight, but come alive at night. You can draw a gargoyle in its stone or "human" form. If you want to draw a "human" gargoyle as in this project, consider adding horns, fangs, claws, heavy brow ridges, beaks, wings, tails, and hooves. Look to existing animals for ideas—the more exotic the animal, the better!

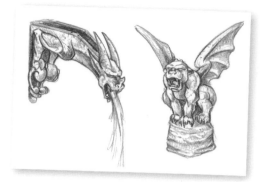

Architectural Differences In architecture, the term *gargoyle* refers to carved water spouts that direct excess water off rooftops (left). Non-functional statues of these beasts are called "grotesques" (right). Try your hand at drawing both!

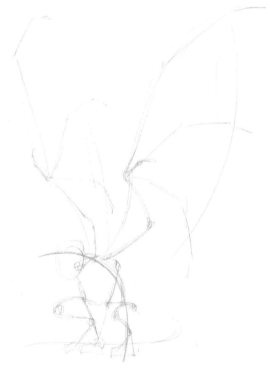

◄ **Step 1** Using an HB pencil, I draw the line of action and roughly indicate the figure, including the tail and wings. I want this gargoyle to be crouching as if he's lurking on the edge of a rooftop with his wings raised above him, so it's important that I establish where his body and wings will be from the start.

▶ **Step 2** Now I use basic shapes to develop the forms. I want to emphasize that the figure is hunched over, so I place the head low on the body and make the shoulders quite bulky. He's shaping up to be pretty muscular, so I'm generous with the muscles in the wings for consistency. I like where I've placed his wing "fingers," so I indicate the curve of the wing membrane stretched between them. Note that the gargoyle's feet are slightly larger than a human's would be; they're more like the paws of a lion or tiger.

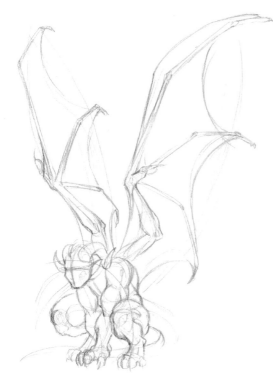

◄ Step 3 Once I'm happy with the basic shape of my gargoyle, I further define the form by indicating specific muscles and adding details like fingers, toes, horns, and a suggestion of the hair. I also sketch guidelines on the head to determine where to place the eyes.

▲ Step 4 After cleaning up a few of my messier sketch lines, I use an HB pencil to draw most of the facial features, including the eyes, nose, mouth, shaggy eyebrows, and a long patch of hair between a pair of spikes on the chin. I also add the pointy ears and a small earring. Next I draw the claws on the feet and wings, the ridges on the horns, and the spikes on the tail.

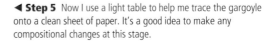

◄ Step 5 Now I use a light table to help me trace the gargoyle onto a clean sheet of paper. It's a good idea to make any compositional changes at this stage.

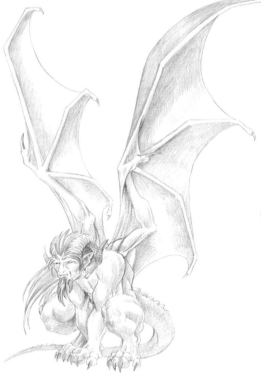

◄ Step 6 Still using the HB pencil, I add shadows with light hatching, just to establish the areas of light and shadow. Later I will fill in areas I want to be darker, such as the hair and the length of tail behind the body.

▶ Step 7 Now I use a softer 2B pencil to go over the areas I want to be darker, such as under the folds of the wings, the backs of the thighs, the area where the leg on the left bends, and the claws. I switch back to the HB to lightly blend some of the darker shadows into the lighters areas; I also shade the rest of the wings with light crosshatching and gradating. Next I shade the hair and goatee, using long strokes that follow the growth of the hair. I keep the tail smooth and without much detail so it doesn't detract from the rest of the figure.

Drawing Stonelike Skin

When a gargoyle comes to life, does the stone transform to flesh? Or does its skin simply look like stone? As the artist, that decision is entirely up to you. Creating the appearance of stonelike skin may seem daunting. Is it enough to shade the entire figure evenly so it appears gray? Perhaps. But by closely examining actual statues and various types of stone such as marble or granite, you'll find many fine details and texture qualities that can lend realism to your gargoyle drawings. A gargoyle with scars might look like it has cracks in its hide, as in this example of a shoulder and bicep. Scratches, pitting, veins of different values, and even weather discoloration can spice up a gargoyle's appearance.

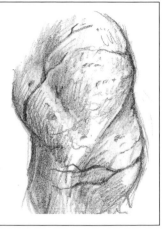

◄ **Step 8** I continue using the 2B pencil to darken some shadows; then I blend them into lighter areas with the HB. Now I use a 4B pencil for the darkest areas, especially underneath the fold of the wings, the ridges of the horns, the hair, and the claws. When darkening the claws, I allow some of the lighter shades and even the white of the paper to show through in a narrow band running the length of each claw. This produces a bright highlight that contrasts with the slick black, making the claw appear shiny. Now I concentrate on the wings, creating their rippled appearance by hatching and lifting out highlights with a kneaded eraser. I also avoid blending my strokes in the wings. Finally, I use the kneaded eraser to lighten the wing on the left, pushing it back into the picture to create depth and make the gargoyle's wingspan look truly grand.

CENTAUR

In Greek mythology, centaurs represent both the best and worst of humans, being half beast and half man. Infamous for being rough and rowdy, centaurs are exceptionally prone to bouts of drunkenness. However, mythology also attributes to some of them a love of knowledge, music, and medicine—a famous centaur named Chiron was a teacher to the Greek hero, Heracles. Centaurs are also superb archers. Artistically, they present a fantastic challenge in combining two of the most difficult creatures to draw—horses and humans. But with a little patience and practice, you can put the two together and have a jolly good time doing it!

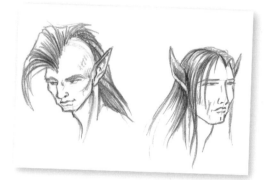

Horsing Around A slightly longer face and nose (right) will make your centaur appear more horselike. Long hair also looks good on a centaur—the hair could grow in a straight line down the scalp, like a horse's mane (left). You can also draw horse ears.

▶ **Step 1** As always, I start by drawing the line of action and sketching the basic figure with an HB pencil. I indicate the hands so they're raised in front of the figure—this is because I want my centaur to be plucking a lyre. I include the bony length of the tail in the sketch to give me an idea of how the rest of the tail will flow. The base of a horse's tail is actually bone—it's the hair that grows from the tail that makes it look long. The position of the tail can say a lot about a horse's (and thus a centaur's) mood— a raised tail usually means excitement or happiness.

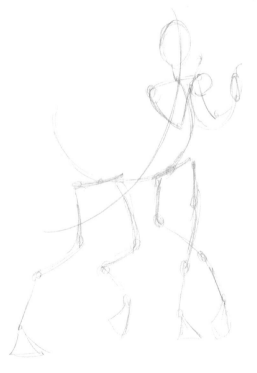

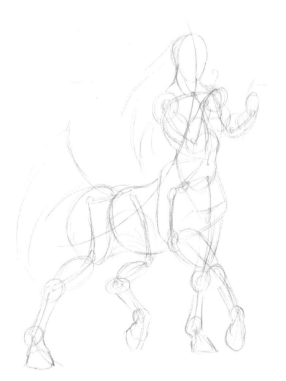

◀ **Step 2** Now I use the HB pencil and simple shapes to develop the forms of the body. I also draw the general shapes of the hair and tail.

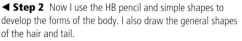

► Step 3 I'm happy with the composition, so I start developing the shapes. I delineate the hooves and fingers, and I block in the eyebrows, nose, mouth, and pointed ears. I also draw the curved lyre between the hands.

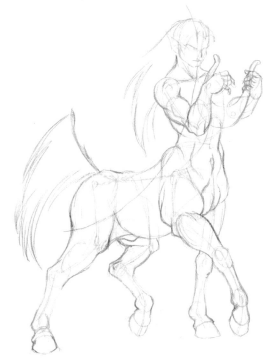

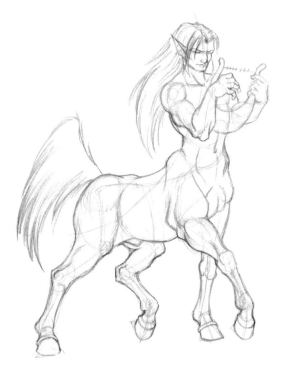

◄ Step 4 Now I create bangs that frame the face, similar to a horse's forelock. I add long strokes to the hair and tail, making them appear wispy. Then I develop the face, adding the eyes and darkening the brows to make him look thoughtful. I also add the crossbar and harp pins to the lyre.

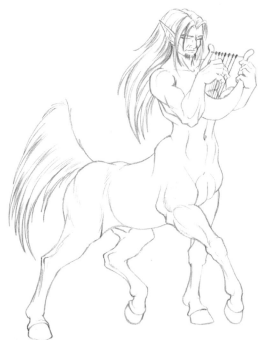

► Step 5 I place my sketch on a light table and transfer the drawing to a clean sheet of paper. As I trace the lines, I decide to add a bit of scruff to the chin, making him look a bit more untamed. I also add strings to the lyre.

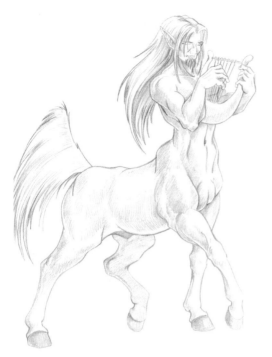

◄ Step 6 Still using the HB pencil, I begin to shade areas of the centaur with light hatchmarks. I add more strokes in the hair and tail, following the direction of hair growth so the hair looks smooth and shiny. Hatching across long hair tends to make it look dull; this is fine for hair that's in shadow, such as the hair behind the centaur's shoulders.

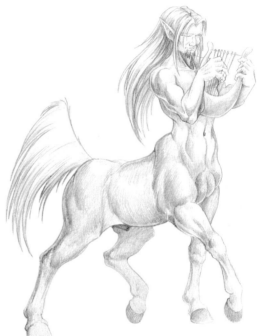

► Step 7 With a 2B pencil, I deepen areas of shadow with more hatching and crosshatching, switching to an HB pencil to blend the darker areas into the surrounding lighter areas with a combination of hatching and gradating. When hatching across a large area like the horse's barrel, I make sure my strokes run crosswise across the form, changing the angle as the form curves to give it depth. Conversely, I keep the shading of the rear leg on the left very flat to suggest distance. Next I use a ruler to draw the strings of the lyre.

Centaur Proportions

Correctly drawing a centaur's proportions can be difficult, as there are few references. Basically, a centaur has the body of a man from the waist up, and the body of a horse from the waist down, with the two halves meeting in the middle. Over time, I've figured out that the horse's shoulders (called "withers") should be positioned where a human's waist is, with the rest of the horse's upper torso replacing what would be human hips. And instead of falling at mid-thigh, a centaur's fingertips should meet the top of the horse's forelegs.

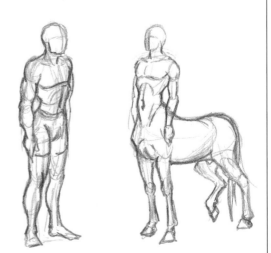

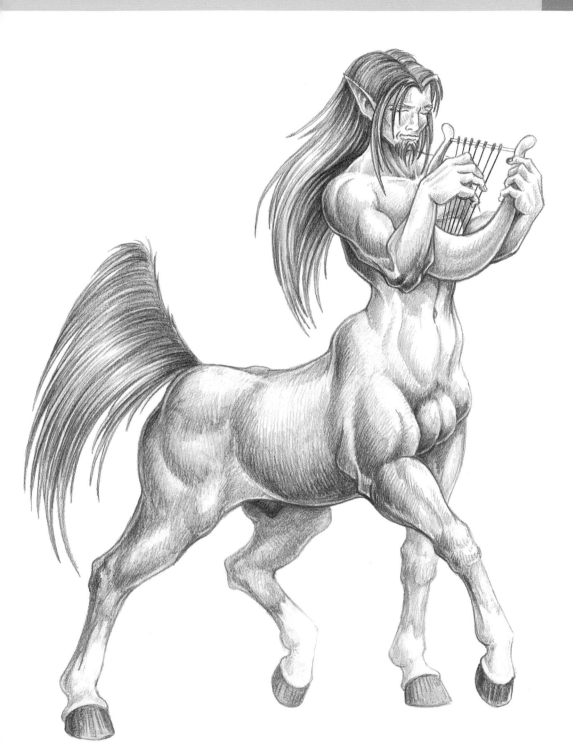

Step 8 I use a soft 4B pencil to push the darkest areas, also using the 2B and HB to blend the dark shadows into the lighter areas. A horse's coat is usually very short and appears smooth from a distance, so I don't want too much detail on the horse's body. But I don't want the centaur to look as if he was carved from stone, so I allow the hatching and crosshatching to imply the texture of the coat. I want the hooves to look shiny, so I use the HB to blend the dark hooves until they look smooth; then I lift out some vertical highlights with a kneaded eraser. I also use the eraser to lift out some of the tone on the fetlocks (the leg area above the hooves), defining the edges of these light areas with the HB. With the 4B, I add darks to the hair and tail, lifting out highlights with the kneaded eraser. Then I add some darker shadows to the hind legs with short, smooth strokes. After darkening the lyre, my centaur is complete.

MERMAID

Mysterious as the ocean itself, mermaids have captured our imaginations for centuries. In folklore, mermaids tend to be mischief makers, often luring sailors to their underwater kingdoms, enchanting them and causing accidents and shipwrecks, and even squeezing the life out of men while trying to rescue them. Some stories, however, portray them as naive creatures who simply forget that humans can't breathe underwater. Whatever the portrayal, mermaids make great visual subjects as they offer endless possibilities in style and design. It's also fun and challenging to create a believable figure that appears to be more than just a fish tail pasted on a human torso.

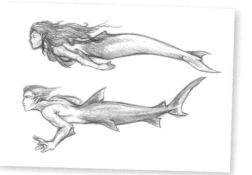

Changing Tails Most merfolk are given tails with horizontally oriented flukes that resemble dolphin's tails in shape and size. However, that doesn't preclude the possibility of giving your merfolk other types of tails, such as shark, eel, octopus, and squid. Note that in the example above the mermaid with the fish tail looks more smooth and fluid than the merman with the shark tail does, but the shark tail is still visually interesting.

▶ **Step 1** I start by drawing a curved line of action to show the mermaid's arched pose; then I build the rough stick figure over it, drawing the arms so that they are raised above the head. I draw a curved line to suggest the length and motion of the tail; the perpendicular line at the end of the tail shows where the tail ends and roughly indicates the angle of the flukes. Notice that I'm being fairly generous with the length of the tail. In terms of proportion, her tail would be at least as long, if not longer, than her legs would be if she were human. Keep this in mind so that your merfolk appear to have sufficient strength and power in their anatomy to propel them through the water.

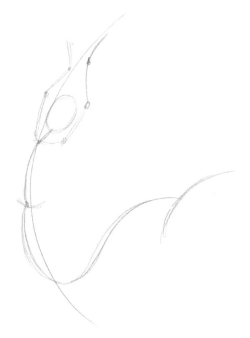

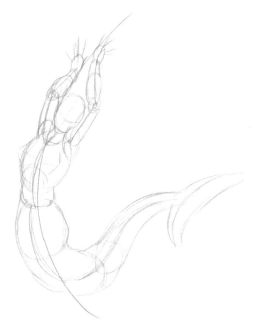

◀ **Step 2** With an HB pencil and basic shapes, I sketch the mermaid's form over the stick figure, using large forms to indicate areas of muscle mass. I consciously avoid making any angles or sharp bends in her tail. The bones of her tail are most likely a continuation of her spine, so a sharp, angular bend in the tail would look unnatural—like a human wearing a mermaid costume. Keeping the curves of the tail smooth visually drives home the point that a mermaid is anatomically different from a land-dwelling human.

▶ **Step 3** When I am satisfied with the overall shape of the figure, I begin to define the forms by sketching specific groups of muscles and curves. I use basic marks to indicate the facial features, draw the flukes of the tail, and add details to her long fingers. Then I block in the general shape of her hair. Because she's suspended in water, I keep my strokes very loose and free to suggest the way the hair floats around her and defies gravity. I don't let myself get too carried away, though, so I draw the hair with somewhat of a downward sweep to show that it still has some weight and buoyancy. Next I draw a rough line to indicate a ridge along the base of her spine and the top of her tail.

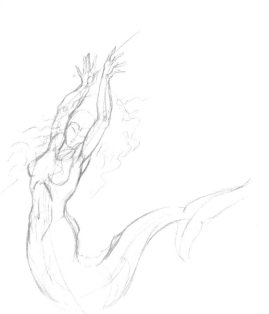

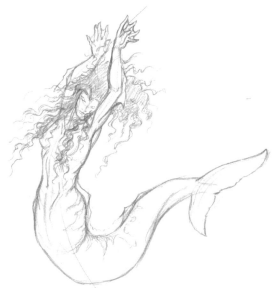

◀ **Step 4** Still using my HB pencil, I further refine the details. I draw the eyes, eyebrows, nose, and mouth, and I refine the shape of her face. I add webbing between her outstretched fingers and sketch fins on her elbows. Then I add more definition to her hair, making it curly. There's a lot of hair, so I add a flat layer of shading to help me keep track of what's there. Next I lightly sketch some loose marks along her tail to suggest the markings.

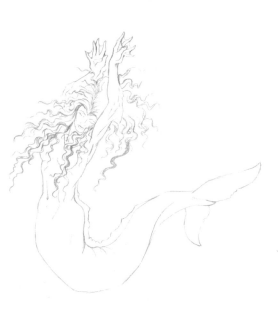

▶ **Step 5** When I'm happy with my sketch, I use a light table to transfer the lines to a clean sheet of paper. I'm especially careful when transferring the lines for the mermaid's hair. It's probably the most complex part of the image, as there are so many lines for the different bunches of hair. This requires a lot of patience, so I take my time with it. I omit the markings on the tail for now because I want to lay down a base of shading on the tail before rendering the details. I'll use the sketch from step 4 as a reference for the markings later.

◄ Step 6 I clean up my lines a bit and lay down rough shading over the entire figure using an HB pencil. I decide at this point that the mermaid's tail will be smooth like a dolphin, rather than scaly like a fish. Then I shade the hair again, following my sketch from step 4 but making the tone a bit darker. I'm more conscious of the flow and shape of her hair this time, however, so I make my strokes follow the general direction of the hair, and I define the curls a bit. I also shade the ridge on her tail so that it's darker than the rest of the tail.

► Step 7 I continue using an HB pencil to shade the figure, blending and smoothing the tone with a kneaded eraser. I use a softer 2B pencil to darken the hair further, still using strokes that follow the direction of the hair growth to keep it looking smooth. I spend a lot of time on the hair, emphasizing some curls and smoothing out others. Moving to the face, I carefully shade around the features. I also add long fingernails that almost look like claws, and I indicate some folds in the webbing between her fingers. Referring to my sketch in step 4, I use a 2B pencil to create the markings on the torso and tail. I also add some darker areas along the ridge of the tail to give it form and texture.

Incorporating Fishy Features

In addition to giving your creature a tail, it's a good idea to incorporate other fishlike features to make your drawing more believable. Perhaps your creature is naturally bald, which helps it move more easily through water. Or maybe it has fins and frills in lieu of hair, as in the example at near right. You could also try making its ears finlike, as seen on the far right. Consider what kinds of markings your creature will have—looking at pictures of tropical fish will provide inspiration. The more you let Mother Nature's influence touch your work, the more believable and natural your creatures will seem.

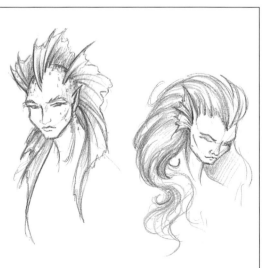

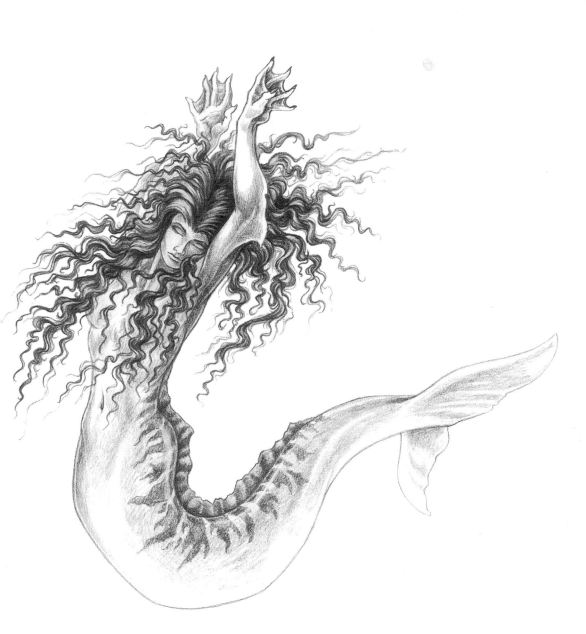

Step 8 I continue to use the HB and 2B pencils to refine the shading on the tail, which is darker on top and fades into white on the underside. I use a kneaded eraser and the HB pencil to shade the lightest areas, and I use the 2B to blend the tone into the darker shadows. Returning to the hair, I use the 2B pencil and an even softer 4B pencil to make the hair even darker, deepening the shadows in the curls. Then I use a kneaded eraser and a very small plastic stick eraser to lift out some highlights in the hair. Using the 2B and HB pencils, I add more floating tendrils of hair, which helps make the hair look less like a solid mass. Next I use the 2B pencil to darken the markings on the torso and tail, adding shadows where they follow the curve of her body. I mold a kneaded eraser into a narrow wedge shape and carefully lift out a line along the top edge of the tail to show where the light is hitting. Then I use the small stick eraser to erase a very fine line where the brightest highlight hits, making the tail look slick and shiny. Finally, I use the 2B pencil to create the deepest shadows on the ridge of the tail, and I use an eraser to lift out some very light highlights on the ridge.

MINOTAUR

Half bull and half man, the Minotaur was a savage, carnivorous monster born of King Minos's wife and a bull that Minos stole from the sea god Poseidon. To punish Minos, Poseidon made Minos's wife fall in love with the bull, which resulted in the birth of the Minotaur. The monster caused so much destruction on the island of Crete that Minos had the architect Daedalus build an elaborate labyrinth to contain the beast, who was ultimately slain by the Greek hero Theseus. In contemporary fiction and games, minotaurs are usually cast as villains, but they are also considered very intelligent and sometimes play the role of the hero.

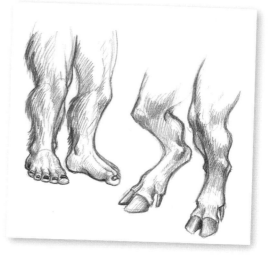

Creating the Feet and Legs My favorite method of drawing minotaur feet is to draw human feet that end in bovine hooves. Instead of a human heel I draw the hock, which leads down into the canon bone and split hoof. Minotaurs still have very human thighs, and their shins are somewhere in between. The end result is usually a bent-legged stance.

◄ **Step 1** I start by drawing the line of action with an HB pencil; then I roughly sketch the rest of the figure. I want the figure to be slightly stooped over, so I indicate this in my sketch. I also indicate a long staff with a straight line.

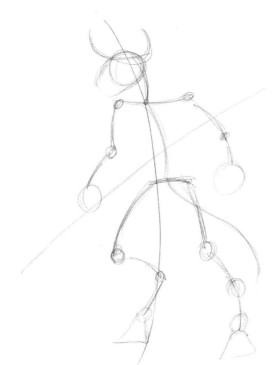

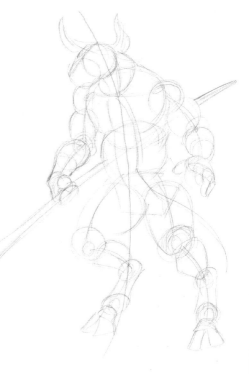

▶ **Step 2** Still using my HB pencil, I start to develop the forms using simple shapes. Note that I give the minotaur a considerable paunch although he's muscular; this is because bulls are powerful yet stocky creatures. Another typical characteristic of hoofed animals is the pair of vestigial dew-claws behind the two main halves of the hoof, which gives the animal the appearance of having four toes. In this vein, I give the minotaur four fingers on his open hand.

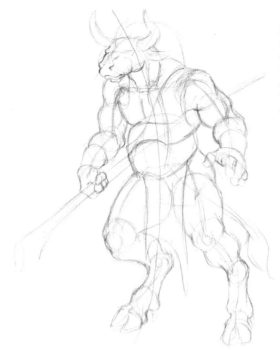

◄ Step 3 I go back over the basic shapes, refining them into more specific details such as the muscles, knees, ankles, nose, mouth, and brow. I also rough in the hair and clothing, which consists of a broad belt over a loincloth and a draped shirt. Next I make the staff thicker at one end, tapering it down to a point at the other end. I also add a tuft of long hair to the end of the tail. Then I develop the hooves, keeping in mind the four-toed appearance of hoofed animals.

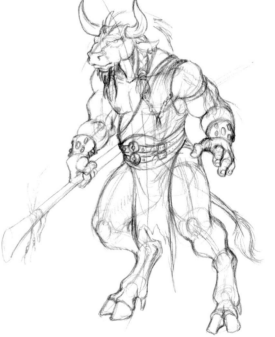

► Step 4 Now that I have the basic form down, I launch a full assault on the details, including the scraggly hair and beard, tattered clothing, and accessories such as the studded wrist bracers, belt, and earrings. I also add the wrapping around the top of his staff, which includes two feathers and strings of beads.

Blending the Features

Because a minotaur is half bull and half man, it's important that the different features blend cohesively; otherwise your creature will look like he's been cut and pasted. One trick I like to use is placing the eyes closer together on the head instead of placing them far apart as you'd see on a cow; this makes the face appear more human. I also draw the lips so they're fuller and more fleshy, making them look capable of speech and expression. Adding long hair on the head can help too.

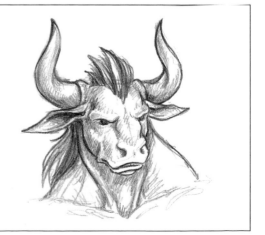

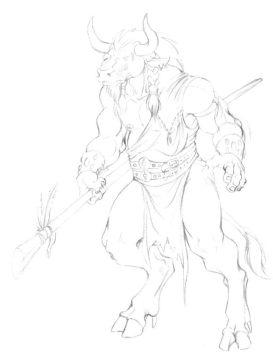

◄ Step 5 Once I've worked out all the details, I use a light table to help me transfer my drawing to a clean sheet of paper. As I trace the lines, I refine the knuckles a bit. I also omit the beads hanging from the staff—they felt like an afterthought in my sketch, so I leave them out of the final drawing.

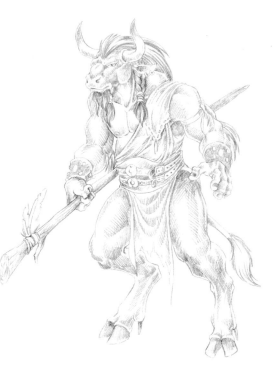

► Step 6 I use the HB pencil to lay down some shading with quick hatching. I work over the entire drawing to plan my light and dark areas. At this point I change the beard a little, splitting it into two "tails." Pairs and split objects are a theme in this composition—the staff and hooves are split; there are two feathers, two braids, two belts, and two earrings; and so on.

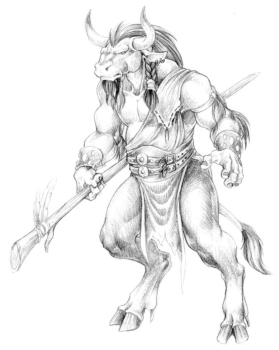

◄ Step 7 When I'm satisfied with my plan for the shading, I use a softer 2B pencil to darken the areas of deepest shadow and the HB pencil to blend the shadowed areas into the lighter areas. I still use hatching to lay down general areas of shadow, and I use softer, smoother strokes for blending. Note, however, that I don't totally eliminate my hatching, leaving some of it to imply the texture of the skin and clothes.

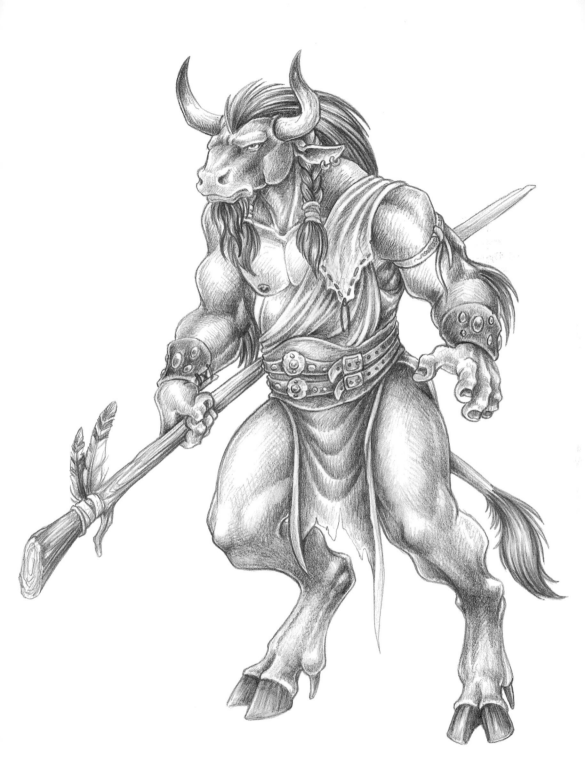

Step 8 I continue shading, still using the 2B pencil for darks and the HB for blending the darks into the lighter areas. I also pay more attention to the clothing, darkening the stitching on the shirt so it stands out against the lighter fabric. I layer deeper values in the hair and beard to make them look even darker. I use vertical strokes on the hooves to make them look slick and smooth but also ridged. I draw tight scribbles on the armband to suggest a tooled or embroidered design. Finally, I create dark tips and bands on the feathers to complement the dark areas on the figure.

SATYR

Half human and half goat, satyrs are known for being wild and carefree. They're also known for their love of spirits—all too fitting, as they are the companions of Dionysus, the Greek god of wine. Revelers by nature, they're often seen playing musical instruments, especially the panpipe. In mythology, satyrs are almost exclusively male—but don't let that put a damper on your creativity.

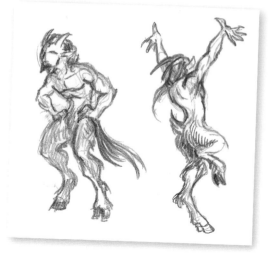

▶ **Satyr Features** Satyrs' legs resemble the hind legs of a goat. They also have goatlike horns and ears, and they usually wear their curly hair and beards long. Some paintings on Greek pottery show satyrs with long horse tails (left), rather than short goat tails (right).

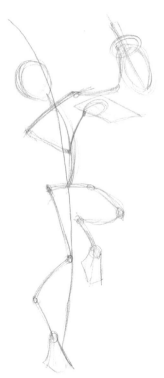

◀ **Step 1** I start by drawing the line of action with an HB pencil; then I work out the placement of the figure. I want my satyr to look happy and carefree, so I place him on one hoof with his head tilted back, as though he's dancing. One arm is raised as if to bring panpipes to his lips or to hold them down as he gives a shout of joy. His other arm is raised up high, holding a bottle of wine. When positioning the legs, I keep in mind that goats and other hoofed animals actually walk on their tiptoes, so I use shapes that reflect this.

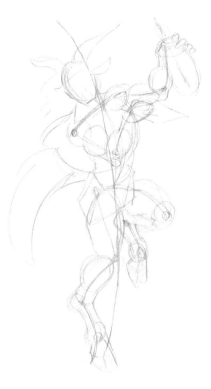

▶ **Step 2** When I'm happy with the pose, I use the HB pencil to develop the forms using basic shapes. I want my satyr to look like he's in motion, prancing about and enjoying himself. To help show this, I position the head as though he's looking back over his shoulder. I decide to give him a horse's tail so that it streams out behind him as he dances. The raised tail shows that he's in high spirits.

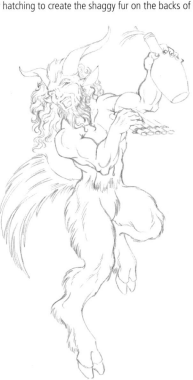

◄ Step 3 Once I have the basic shapes down, I develop the forms of the body, defining the fingers, hooves, wine bottle, and panpipes; then I add the facial features, with the mouth open as if he's shouting with joy, and the goatlike ears. I also suggest the shaggy fur around the hips and fill in the bushy tail. Next I draw a few splashes of liquid from the top of the bottle to suggest movement.

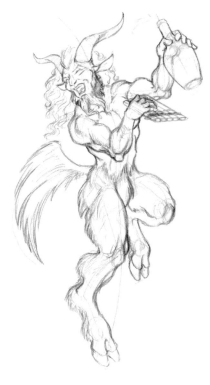

► Step 4 I continue refining the forms and darkening lines with the HB pencil. I notice that the angle of the panpipes is a bit off, so I make the necessary adjustments, including the position of the fingers. Then I add details to the face, hair, beard, and horns. I continue suggesting the fur on the lower half of the body, quickly hatching to create the shaggy fur on the backs of the legs.

◄ Step 5 Once I'm satisfied with the satyr, I place my sketch on a light table and transfer the drawing to a clean sheet of paper.

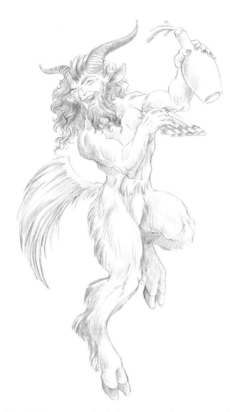

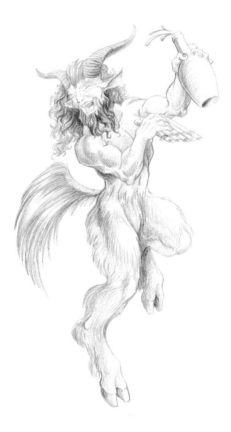

◄ Step 6 Now that I have a clean drawing, I start shading the entire body with the HB pencil and light hatching. To make the legs look like they're covered in long fur, I keep my hatchmarks farther apart from one another, following the curves of the muscles.

► Step 7 Now I create the darkest areas with a 2B pencil, especially concentrating on the hair, tail, and beard. Then I carefully shade the horns to further define the ridges, lifting out highlights here and there with a kneaded eraser. Now I focus on the legs, using widely spaced hatchmarks that follow the shape of the limbs. For darker areas on the legs, such as the area of the leg and foot that are tucked under the raised thigh, I build up layers of hatching. Next I lightly indicate some hair on the satyr's right arm, just to make him look a little more shaggy and wild.

Drawing Horns

Horns are wonderfully varied, and offer a great opportunity for you to get creative. Some horns are smooth and others ridged; some curve back off the head and others point forward or straight up. Horns can also be long and curled or short and pointy. Use the Internet or an encyclopedia to get ideas for different horns for your satyr; you might even want to try combining two types of horns to make your character truly unique.

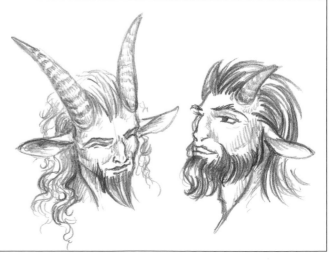

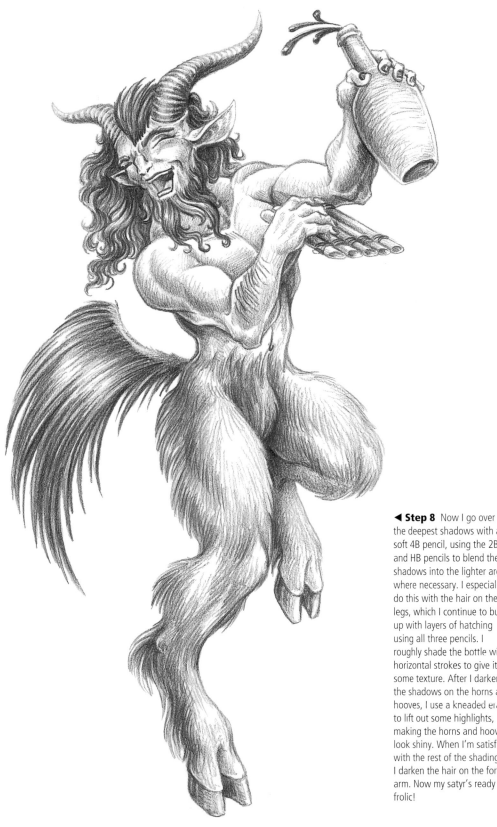

◄ **Step 8** Now I go over
the deepest shadows with a
soft 4B pencil, using the 2B
and HB pencils to blend the
shadows into the lighter areas
where necessary. I especially
do this with the hair on the
legs, which I continue to build
up with layers of hatching
using all three pencils. I
roughly shade the bottle with
horizontal strokes to give it
some texture. After I darken
the shadows on the horns and
hooves, I use a kneaded eraser
to lift out some highlights,
making the horns and hooves
look shiny. When I'm satisfied
with the rest of the shading,
I darken the hair on the forearm. Now my satyr's ready to
frolic!

OGRE

Usually portrayed as huge brutes with more brawn than brains, ogres have been terrorizing humans in folklore and fantasy for quite some time. They're often depicted with a large head, abundant hair, bulging muscles, and a portly belly (probably full of human parts). Although ogres are thought of as large humanoids, there's more to drawing one than enlarging a human and giving it a club. Read on to find out what you can do to make your ogre drawings truly terrifying!

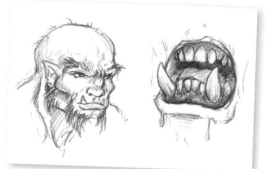

Ogre-fying the Face Try giving your ogre a square, heavy jaw with fangs that protrude over the upper lip. Also try including pointy ears, tufted eyebrows, long facial hair, and angular cheekbones. When drawing the teeth, you may want to make the fangs curve upward and out to enhance the ferociousness. A little drool never hurts, either.

◄ **Step 1** I start with the usual line of action. Even though I plan for this ogre to be standing upright, the line of action curves slightly forward to show his stooped posture. When I sketch the figure, I keep in mind how much bigger the ogre's proportions are than the average human's, so I allow more room for the heaviness of the limbs. I want this character to hold a huge club, so I indicate its placement with a single line.

▶ **Step 2** Now I start to rough in the figure and the club with basic shapes. Note how much different the proportions are from those of an average human: The head is set low, the torso is quite short, and the arms are long and ape-like with enormous hands. The short, somewhat stubby legs help give the impression of considerable size and weight.

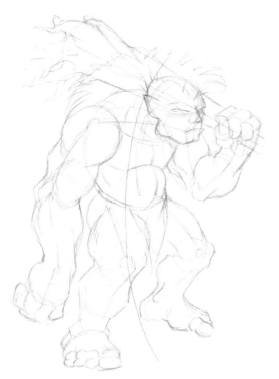

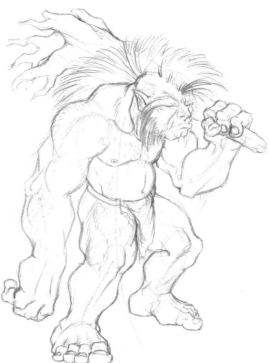

Step 3 Now I start adding details like the facial features, fingers, toes, and loincloth. I also add some details to the club, making it look like the ogre ripped a tree out of the ground to use as a weapon. Instead of giving him a full head of hair, I adorn his head with a row of stiff, spiked hair to make him look more savage. Then I define the muscles and pot belly.

Step 4 I refine the shapes, defining the muscles and adding details such as fingernails, toenails, shaggy facial hair that extends from the eyebrows to the cheeks, and scraggly hair all over the body. I also fill in the beady eyes underneath his heavy eyebrows and add tusklike teeth that jut out over his upper lip. Then I refine his mouth, turning it into a grumpy frown.

Ogre Proportions

When looking at this drawing of a human next to an ogre, size is the most obvious difference. But take a look at the proportions—the human is about six heads tall but the ogre is only about four and a half heads tall, which makes him look incredibly stocky. Like a human, his elbows fall at the waist, but his long forearms and hunched-over stance place his hands near his knees, rather than at mid thigh. Overall, the basic parts of a human are all there, but they're sized differently, which makes all the difference. Your ogres don't need to follow these proportions exactly—use this as a starting place and experiment until you find a look that suits your own vision of an ogre.

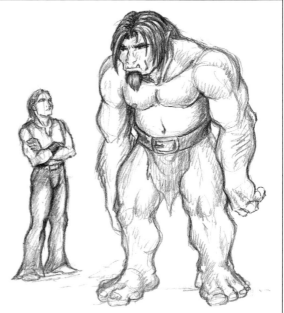

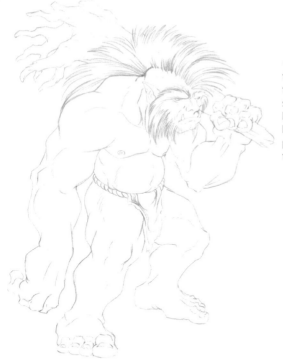

◄ Step 5 When I'm happy with my drawing, I use a light table to transfer the lines onto a clean sheet of drawing paper. When transferring, I keep most of the outlines and details from my sketch, but I omit most of the body hair I added in the last step because I want to shade the entire body before adding the short, bristly hairs. I can reference my sketch later when it's time to place the hair. Next I refine the face a little more and add detail to the twisted rope that's holding up his tattered loincloth.

► Step 6 With an HB pencil, I start establishing the basic shadow areas across the figure, including the club. I keep the shading on the club quite sketchy, making the strokes mostly parallel to the length of the club to suggest bark. Making the hair on the head and face the darkest areas helps keep the club and body separate.

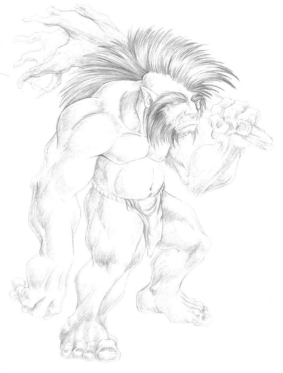

◄ **Step 7** I use a 2B pencil to add darker shadows to the figure, blending these darker areas with the lighter shadows using an HB pencil. I use quite a bit of hatching and crosshatching on the figure, which makes the skin look a bit rough. I also use the 2B pencil to darken the hair even more, using strokes that follow the direction of the hair growth to make it look smooth and shiny. Still using the 2B pencil, I darken the pupils, fingernails, toenails, loincloth, and belt, increasing the contrast for visual interest.

▶ **Step 8** To make the hair look really dark and black, I go over the strokes with a 4B pencil. Then I use the 2B and HB pencils to finish the club, using hatching and crosshatching around the roots to help the bark look rough. I lift out some tone on the farthest roots with a kneaded eraser to make them look more distant (must be a really big club!). I also erase some of the tone on the ogre's left foot to push it back a bit more. After blending and smoothing the shading all over the body with HB and 2B pencils, I sharpen my 2B pencil and start adding the short, bristly hair on the chest, arms, shoulders, legs, and feet. I make his scalp a little more stubbly as well, and I add some bristles to the back of his neck. I sure wouldn't want to run into this guy on a dark mountain trail, that's for sure!

GRYPHON

With the body of a lion and the head, talons, and wings of an eagle, the gryphon was said to protect the Scythian steppes (modern Ukraine, Russia, and Kazakhstan) from anyone who attempted to steal the gold and precious stones that were abundant there. As a result, the gryphon (also known as "griffin") was commonly featured on gold coins in Scythia. Because a gryphon takes a single mate for life, it has become a symbol of fidelity. Visually, this creature presents a unique challenge in that it combines two very different animals into a unique whole.

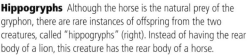

Hippogryphs Although the horse is the natural prey of the gryphon, there are rare instances of offspring from the two creatures, called "hippogryphs" (right). Instead of having the rear body of a lion, this creature has the rear body of a horse.

◄ **Step 1** First I indicate the line of action with an HB pencil. (Remember that the line of action denotes the general movement and flow of the figure, and thus doesn't need to be in line with the spine.) I want to show off this gryphon's wings, so I include the wing bones in my initial sketch.

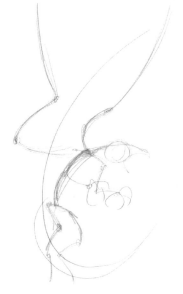

▶ **Step 2** Now I start to build up the figure with basic forms. I use wide, sweeping arcs to indicate the placement of the wings. Note how big the wings are—this follows the rule of thumb that a creature's wingspan should be at least two times the length of the body.

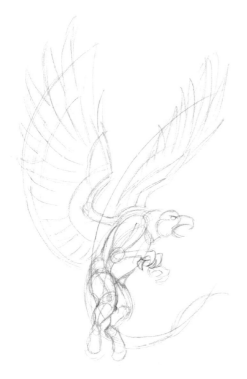

◄ Step 3 When I'm satisfied with the rough forms, I add details, mostly to the wings. I pay most attention to the long primary feathers because they're the largest parts of the wing. Note that the wing on the left is facing the viewer, and the wing on the right is angled slightly away. Feathered wings can be very difficult to draw from any angle, so using reference photos of winged animals can be invaluable. To show that the wing is on the downstroke, I curve back the lines for the primary feathers so they look like they're resisting the movement through the air. For now, I indicate groups of smaller feathers with simple shapes.

► Step 4 Still using the HB pencil, I start working in the finer details from head to tail. I tighten up the shapes of the beak and tongue, create brow ridges that end in tufted feathers, define the curved talons, indicate the lion's paws, and draw the hair at the end of the tail. I also detail the wings, indicating smaller feathers with short, curved lines.

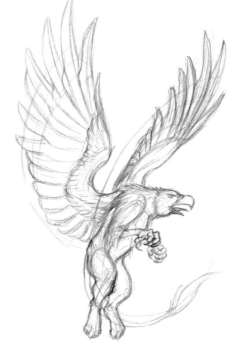

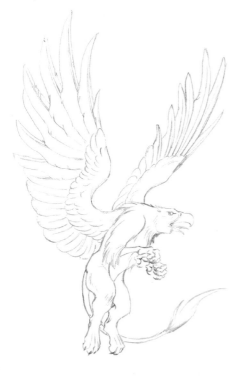

◄ Step 5 When I'm satisfied with the sketch, I take it to my light table and transfer the drawing to a clean sheet of paper. As I transfer, I indicate the main shaft on most of the larger feathers; I also draw some short lines to show clumps or gaps in the barbs—the parts of the feather that branch off from the main shaft.

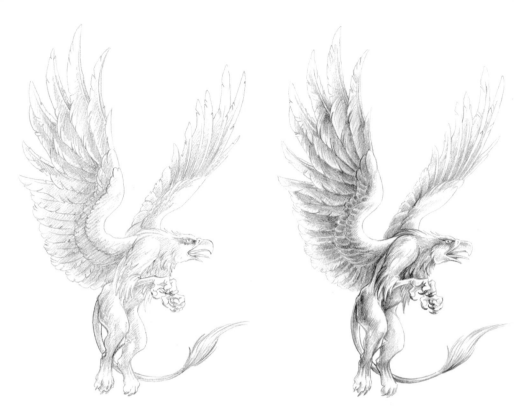

Step 6 Using hatching and the HB pencil, I establish the basic shadow areas across the drawing. When working on the larger feathers, I make sure my strokes follow the direction of the barbs; this will help indicate the feathers' texture and even suggest movement.

Step 7 Switching to a 2B pencil, I darken the deepest shadow areas by hatching. To blend the shadows into the lighter areas, I use the HB pencil and soft strokes. I spend a considerable amount of time detailing the large feathers; the small feathers are less detailed, but I keep their edges white so they stand out.

Combining Anatomical Parts

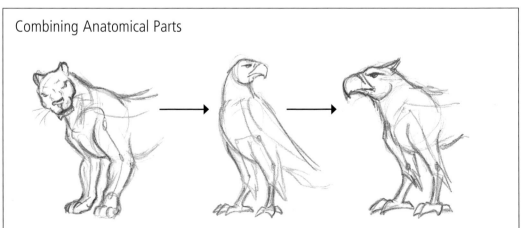

When combining aspects of a lion and an eagle to yield a gryphon, the lion's forelegs are effectively replaced with the hind legs of the eagle—as with all birds, an eagle's forelegs are its wings. The trick to drawing a convincing gryphon is in reassociating the disparate parts of its anatomy. The lion's "elbows" become the "heel" of the eagle's leg, and the eagle's "ankle" becomes the lion's "wrist." Keep these parallels in mind when constructing your gryphon.

▶ **Step 8** Now I use the softer 2B pencil to darken the shadows, especially on the wings and face. I return to the HB occasionally for blending darker areas into lighter ones. I make good use of my kneaded eraser, lifting out highlights and lightening the tips of the wing on the right, making it seem farther away from the viewer. I take a step back from my drawing and make any necessary adjustments; then my gryphon is complete!

NIGHTMARE

Most of us think of nightmares as scary dreams, not fantasy creatures. The idea of a nightmare as a mystical horse is a fairly recent notion, but the fiery black creature has become popular in contemporary fiction and games as an antagonist or hostile spirit (true to its name). The most striking feature of the nightmare is that its mane and tail are composed of fire. Sometimes the creature is credited as breathing fire, blowing smoke from its nostrils, or even having flaming hooves. Fire can be a challenge to draw, so this lesson will explore adapting flames to work convincingly in place of hair.

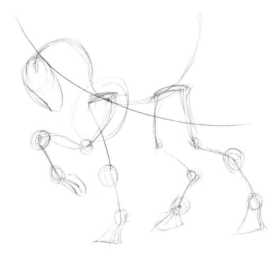

◀ **Step 1** As usual, I draw the line of action first with an HB pencil. In this case, it's a fairly simple arch, as I want to convey a powerful forward motion. I build up the lines of the figure to reflect this stance, with the neck arched and the closest foreleg lifted up—almost like the parade step of a well-trained dressage horse. Although I want my creature to convey a sense of elegance, I also want her to seem solid and powerful, like a heavy draft horse. To do this, I make her back a little shorter than a typical horse's, making her seem more compact.

▶ **Step 2** Now I use basic shapes to develop the forms. I use large shapes for the mane and tail, providing room for the flames. I also draw long ears—a horse usually has smaller ears, but I want to suggest that this nightmare is associated with death, so I give her ears that resemble the jackal-headed Egyptian god of death and judgment, Anubis.

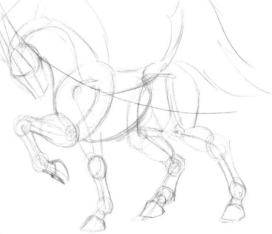

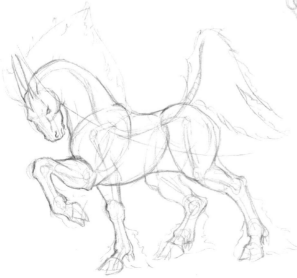

◀ **Step 3** Still using the HB pencil, I add more form to the muscles, making them look heavy and solid. I also add details to the face, such as the eyes, mouth, and nostrils. I indicate some flames on the edges of the mane and tail, and I add some flames around the hooves. I decide to make her hooves split like a cow's—this makes her look otherworldly (as horses have solid hooves), and a bit scary, as we tend to associate split hooves with demons. I also start to indicate some of the bones of her tail.

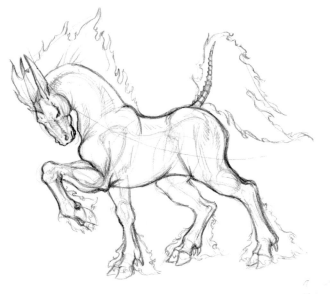

◄ Step 4 I like the direction I am taking with this drawing, so I keep adding details. I indicate the indlvldual bones ın her tail, more clearly define the shape of the flames, and render the muscles in more detail.

▶ Step 5 Now I use my light table to transfer the lines I want to keep to a clean sheet of paper. I'm especially careful with the outline of the flames, drawing just light enough so I can see them. Because I know I want to keep the trailing edge of the flames light, it's better to keep them light now and darken them later, rather than trying to lighten up dark lines.

◄ Step 6 Using the HB pencil, I create the basic shadow areas with hatching. Because her coat is black, I'm not afraid to allow some of the areas to become darker than others across her body. Conversely, I'm very careful with the flames, only adding the lightest shading at the base for now.

Creating the Flames

When replacing what would be a "normal" horse's mane, tail, and hooves with a nightmare's fiery flames, it's a good idea to use the real animal's traits as a tool for comparison, as illustrated below.

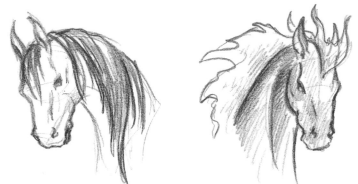

▲ **Mane** I've found that the mane is the easiest quality to interpret as flames. Because a horse's mane follows a simple line down the arch of its neck, it's fairly clear where the fire will start on a nightmare. Arranging the flames as they lick upward from the neck has the interesting effect of always implying movement, even if the nightmare is standing still. Look at photos of horses in motion, especially those that are running; when the wind blows through the mane, it often resembles flickering flames. Keep this in mind, and let it be your inspiration.

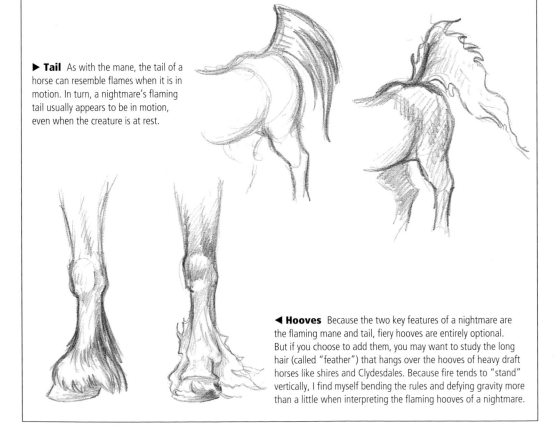

▶ **Tail** As with the mane, the tail of a horse can resemble flames when it is in motion. In turn, a nightmare's flaming tail usually appears to be in motion, even when the creature is at rest.

◀ **Hooves** Because the two key features of a nightmare are the flaming mane and tail, fiery hooves are entirely optional. But if you choose to add them, you may want to study the long hair (called "feather") that hangs over the hooves of heavy draft horses like shires and Clydesdales. Because fire tends to "stand" vertically, I find myself bending the rules and defying gravity more than a little when interpreting the flaming hooves of a nightmare.

◄ **Step 7** Now I change my method of shading to be very deliberate and careful. Though I start to use a softer 2B pencil as usual, I must keep in mind a very complicated lighting situation—the figure's mane, tail, and hooves are all on fire! This has the effect of illuminating the figure from six different angles. Just as I darken the base of the flames a bit more, the edges of the forms adjacent to the base of the flames are lightest. This is especially noticeable around the feet, which are surrounded by flames and thus are most illuminated. Notice that I leave a light area along the underside of the belly and the bottom of the raised foreleg to show illumination. Finally, I add more details to the trailing edges of the flames. I'm very careful to keep the edges light, but I also let the lines "read" as delicate, wispy tendrils.

► **Step 8** To convey the darks of the black coat, I use softer pencils such as 3B and 4B. I use a kneaded eraser and a small stick eraser to lift out highlights along the neck, haunches, and the bottom of the raised leg. I also use the kneaded eraser to lighten the two back legs so they seem more distant. I add a few more darks to the base of the flames, giving them more dimension. I shade the ear on the other side of the mane just enough to make it visible through the flames, and I add more flames to the tail, covering the ridges at the top of the tailbone. Finally, I shade the eye. I saved this for last because it could make or break the drawing—and she does look appropriately mean!

UNICORN

If dragons are an archetypal fantasy creature from one end of the spectrum, unicorns are their counterpart, being equally recognized and popular throughout history, literature, and now film and television. It is quite possible that no two fantasy creatures are as instantly recognizable.

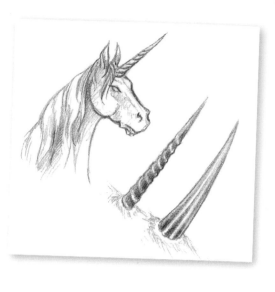

▶ **Horns** The primary feature that sets unicorns apart from mundane horses is their single horn, properly called an "alicorn." It is commonly whorled or spiraled, but don't let that hamper your creativity. The world is full of horned creatures of various forms, some with very spectacular (or at least detailed and interesting) horns. Study what exists, and let those images inspire you when it's time to create something fantastic.

◀ **Step 1** I start by drawing the line of action with an HB pencil; then I block in the lines of the figure. Although the pose is fairly static and stately, I add some motion to the composition by drawing the head so the unicorn is looking back over its shoulder.

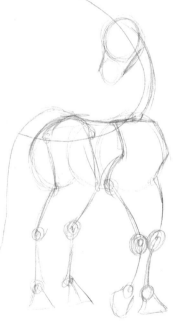

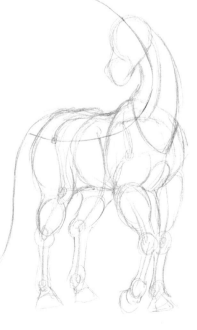

▶ **Step 2** When I'm satisfied with the pose, I start to round out the figure with basic shapes. You've probably noticed that I haven't added the alicorn yet; I'm saving my favorite part for the next step!

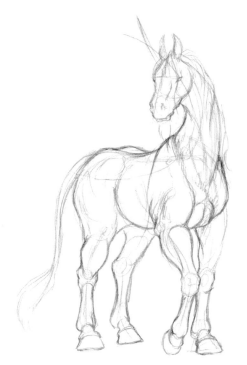

◄ Step 3 Still sketching with the HB pencil, I start fleshing out more of the details: I define the muscles, add the mane and tuft of hair at the end of the tail, and draw the goatlike beard on the chin. I also add the ears, eyes, nose, mouth, and alicorn. Because the nightmare seemed so otherworldly, I choose to make the unicorn a little more "earthy" by drawing solid (not split) hooves and a slightly curved alicorn.

► Step 4 Now I concentrate on the hair: I indicate the way the mane falls in layers, add hair to the fetlocks, and create the long forelock that falls to either side of the alicorn. I also detail the alicorn, making it ridged rather than smooth or spiraled. Next I lay down hatching that follows the contours of the muscles, especially around the neck.

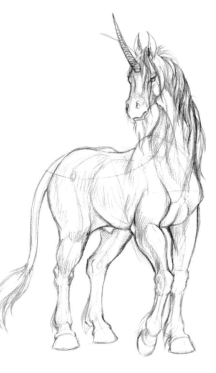

◄ Step 5 This composition is very simple, but I'm pleased with how it's going. I use the light table to help transfer most of my lines—along with some of the hatching to keep track of the contours of the muscles—to a clean sheet of paper.

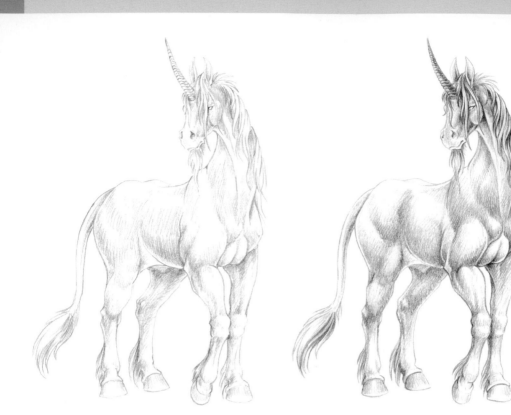

Step 6 Now I use the HB pencil and hatching to indicate the general shading across the unicorn. For the long hair, I use strokes that run parallel to the direction of the hair growth; this makes the hair look smooth and silky.

Step 7 I want to keep the image fairly light, implying a white or very light coat, so when I darken the shadows in this step I continue using the HB pencil instead of switching to a softer 2B. I slowly build up the shading with layers of hatching, gently blending with short, smooth strokes. I keep the shading on the alicorn and hooves smooth and subtle. To make the hooves look polished, I use a combination of vertical strokes and strokes that follow the shape of the hoof.

Unicorn Variations

Besides the alicorn, another common feature of the unicorn is a lion's tail, rather than a traditional horse's tail. Some unicorns also have split hooves, rather than solid ones.

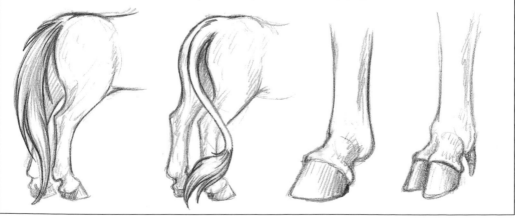

▶ **Step 8** Now I bring in a soft 2B pencil to darken some of the deepest shadows, especially the alicorn, hooves, and darkest strands of hair. Overall, the effect is very subtle, making the figure seem aloof and distant, true to the mythology surrounding this species.

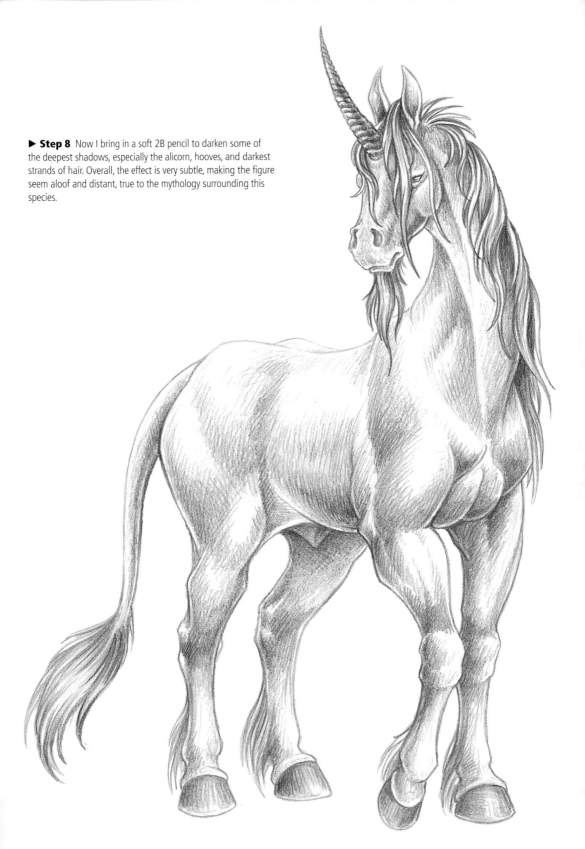

DRAGON DUEL

Up to this point, I've described how individual
creatures are put together and outlined some
points to consider when deciding how those
creatures look and move when you draw them.
But what happens when two creatures meet?
Specifically, what happens when two dragons
clash over territory, gold (which dragons adore),
or today's damsel in distress? Of course, not all
dragons are aggressive, and not all of them will
pick a fight when they meet another dragon.
But if they do, what might that encounter look
like? This project is my interpretation of an aerial
dragon fight—the figures aren't limited by having
to maintain their footing, so they're free to twist
and turn around each other in space.

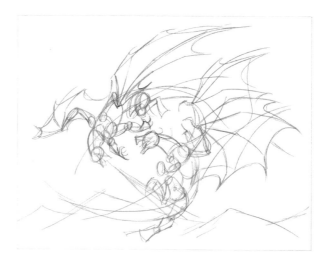

Sketching the Composition The first thing I do is go to my
sketchbook and work out several ideas for the composition. The
one I settled on has a circular flow and gives a sense of the motion
of the two dragons tumbling through the air, constantly circling
each other.

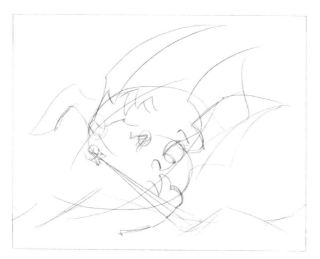

◄ **Step 1** Even though I'll transfer my
initial sketch to a clean sheet of paper
later, I start by using a ruler to mark
borders on the page. This will help me
keep the composition centered the way
I want it. Also, leaving a border around
your drawing makes the image look
more polished, and it makes it easier
to get the final matted and framed.
Because there are two figures in this
scene, each one gets a line of action.
Referring to my original sketch, I block in
the stick figures, wings, and the plume of
fire from the dragon on the left. I sketch
some mountaintops below the figures to
indicate that the dragons are in mid-air.

▶ **Step 2** Next I block in the forms
with simple shapes, using the framework
of the stick figures. Notice that I "draw
through" in places—this helps me make
sure that the limbs are attached and
positioned correctly, even though we
might not be able to see them later on.

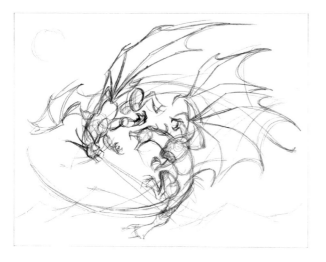

◄ **Step 3** Once I've established the basic shapes, I add a little more detail, such as toes, ears, horns, and whiskers. I add more definition to the wings, and I use a few loose circles to indicate the sun's position in the upper-left corner.

► **Step 4** Now I add even more detail, including claws, eyes, and the shape of the flames. The dragon on the right gets a long row of spikes down his back and tail, and the dragon on the left has what looks like a fin running the length of his body. The dragon on the right also gets some tattered edges on his wings. If you look closely at the dragon on the left, you'll see two little slashes that indicate fresh wounds. I don't detail the right forearm of the dragon on the right because I will omit the limb entirely when I transfer the drawing in the next step. This is because it is mostly obscured by the dragon's wing and we can assume the limb is there.

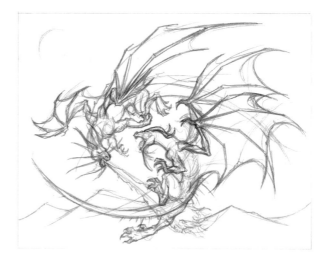

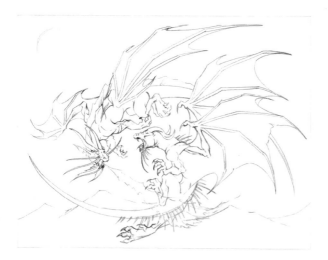

◄ **Step 5** Now I mark the correct borders on a new sheet of drawing paper and use my light table to transfer the sketch. As I trace the lines of the sketch, I make sure the details are nice and crisp. I also add more spikes to the dragon on the right, extending them to his shoulders and the base of his neck. Note that I also transfer the light outline for the placement of the sun.

▶ **Step 6** Before I start shading, I mark off the borders on the page with artist's tape. I place the tape with one edge right up against the border lines I marked, extending the tape about an inch or two beyond the paper edges on all sides. When I remove the tape in the last step, I'll have clean, neat edges. Now I use an HB pencil to start indicating the light and dark areas of the composition. The lightest areas are those that are most brightly illuminated by the flames. I create a few darker areas throughout, especially around the dragon's heads—this helps keep things separate and clearly defined. Don't be afraid to

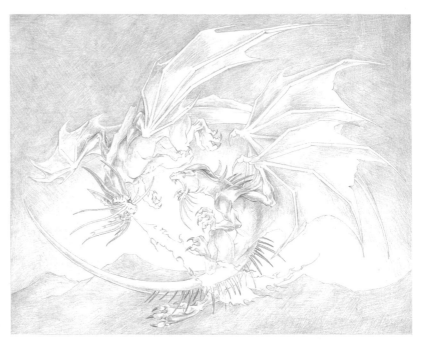

do this wherever you need to, especially in a busy scene such as this one; it'll help you keep track of all your details. Just be careful not to go too dark at this stage, because you might change your mind later. For the sky, I use a harder F pencil to keep the shading very light, especially toward the horizon. I make the sky darker near the top of the image and lighter toward the horizon; if you look outside on a clear day, you'll notice the same effect. I take a lot of time when shading the sky, building up layers to smooth out the shading as much as I can. Notice that I shaded over the sun—I'll explain this in the final step.

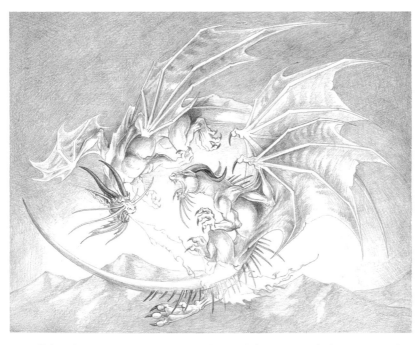

◀ **Step 7** I continue to darken the sky by adding more layers with an F pencil; then I smooth out the shading with an HB. I vary the length and direction of my marks as I build up more layers, which helps smooth the shading and obscure the underlying pencil marks. Next I use some light hatching and crosshatching to add texture and folds to the wings of both dragons and to the finlike ridge along the spine of the dragon on the left. I make the mountains a little bit darker, and I use a kneaded eraser to pick out some lighter areas along the mountaintops. Even though I'm indicating

areas of light and shadow on the mountains, I keep them very light, using atmospheric perspective to show that they are in the distance. Notice that I haven't done much shading in the areas behind the flames for now—this is because the flames will be one of the last things I add detail to, as I'll explain in the next step.

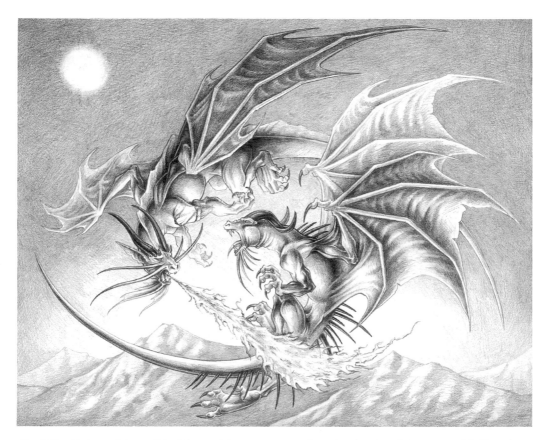

Step 8 Now it's time to darken and blend the rest of the shadows. I make some of the shadows quite dark, especially in areas that are farthest away from the flames, such as along the backside, wings, and tail of the dragon on the left. This high-contrast shading helps make the lighting from the flames seem more dramatic. To build the darkest darks, I apply several layers of shading with the HB pencil and then layer over it with a 2B, switching again to the HB to blend the shadows back into the lighter areas. Because this is a daylight scene, I employ atmospheric perspective to the farthest wing of the dragon on the left, making it look even farther away. I use a similar trick with the dragon on the right, making his left wing appear closer by giving it more detail. Next I add more detail and shading to the mountains, making the center range the darkest and most detailed. Then I

create the sun by using a kneaded eraser to carefully lift out the graphite in a circular shape—the result has a very soft edge, giving the sun a soft, glowing appearance. I add a third wound to the shoulder of the dragon on the left, adding a few trickles to indicate gore. Finally, I concentrate on the fire. To achieve the rough, chaotic appearance of the flames, I lightly scribble with the F and HB pencils, making the base and center column of the flames the darkest areas. Then, using a kneaded eraser and a small stick eraser, I lift out the tips of some of the flames and add bright highlights all over. To finish, I use the tip of a sharp HB pencil to pick out some of the edges of the flames, taking care not to press too hard or etch the lines into the page. Once I'm finished, I very slowly and carefully peel off the artist's tape to reveal my crisp, clean borders. There you have it—a great dragon duel!

CLOSING WORDS

If you heed the call of the fantastic, look for the unbelievable in the most mundane things around you. Take a sketchbook everywhere. Draw your friends; people on the bus; animals at the zoo; that crazy creature with an elephant's ears, ram's horns, and a horse's tail on a wolf's body that you swear you saw out of the corner of your eye. How does your subject fit together? How does it move? What does it do in its environment? Consider the answers to these questions, and you'll find ways to make that crazy critter look mighty convincing when you put it down on paper.

Don't be dismayed when things don't work out. Sometimes you have to make some mistakes before you find what works for you. That's the funny thing about art—it works differently for everyone. I've had some really good teachers who reminded me of that, and some not-so-good ones who insisted that their way was the only way. (I've since learned to take a grain of salt with advice given by a person who only paints metal trash cans and chain-link fences). Learn to adapt to situations when you have to, but keep that rebellious streak carefully hidden in your pocket and pull it out when no one is looking.

The techniques in this book are what work for me today. They might not work for me tomorrow, because artists are funny that way. If the things I've described work for you, use them. If they don't, feel free to toss them out. If my ideas have at least given you a solid place to start from, then I consider this endeavor a success.

Keep exploring. Experiment until you find what works best, then try to make it even better. With that in mind (and a healthy sense of adventure and wonder), you'll find that anything is possible.

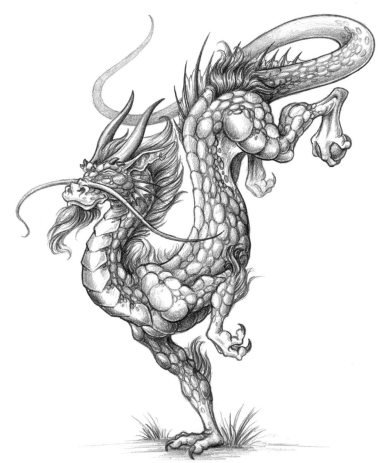